# MARCO POLO

# BARBADOS

**with Local Tips**

*The author's special recommendations are*
*highlighted in yellow throughout this guide*

D0369338

*There are five symbols to help you find your way around this guide:*

*Marco Polo's top recommendations – the best in each category*

*sites with a scenic view*

*places where the local people meet*

*places where young people get together*

**(100/A1)**
*pages and coordinates for the Road Atlas of Barbados*
**(U/A1)** *coordinates for the City Map of Bridgetown inside back cover*

# MARCO ⊕ POLO

*Travel guides and language guides in this series:*

Alaska • Algarve • Amsterdam • Australia/Sydney • Bahamas • Barbados
Berlin • Brittany • California • Canada • Channel Islands • Costa
Brava/Barcelona • Costa del Sol/Granada • Côte d'Azur • Crete • Cuba
Cyprus • Dominican Republic • Eastern Canada • Eastern USA • Florence
Florida • Gran Canaria • Greek Islands/Aegean • Ibiza/Formentera • Ireland
Istanbul • Lanzarote • London • Mallorca • Malta • Mexico • New York
New Zealand • Normandy • Paris • Prague • Rhodes • Rome • San Francisco
Scotland • South Africa • Southwestern USA • Tenerife • Turkish Coast
Tuscany • USA: Southern States • Venice • Western Canada

French • German • Italian • Spanish

*Marco Polo would be very interested to hear your*
*comments and suggestions. Please write to:*

*North America:*
Marco Polo North America
70 Bloor Street East
Oshawa, Ontario, Canada
(B) 905-436-2525

*United Kingdom:*
GeoCenter International Ltd
The Viables Centre
Harrow Way
Basingstoke, Hants RG22 4BJ

*Our authors have done their research very carefully, but should any errors or omissions*
*have occurred, the publisher cannot be held responsible for any injury, damage*
*or inconvenience suffered due to incorrect information in this guide*

*Cover photograph: Eastcoast near Bathsheba (Huber)*
*Photos: Author (4, 7, 16, 22, 24, 26, 28, 31, 37, 42, 48, 50, 57, 58, 61, 64, 68, 73, 74, 76, 79, 82);*
*Mauritius: Hubatka (99), Mac Laren (19), Messerschmidt (32), Pearce (53, 54),*
*Torino (80), Vidler (66); Schuster: Harding (38), Indra (9), Tovy (12).*

*1ˢᵗ edition 2000*
*© Mairs Geographischer Verlag, Ostfildern, Germany*
*Author: Uschi Wetzels*
*Translator: Dennis Brehme*
*English edition 2000: Gaia Text*
*Editorial director: Ferdinand Ranft*
*Chief editor: Marion Zorn*
*Cartography for the Road Atlas: © Berndtson & Berndtson, Fürstenfeldbruck*
*Design and layout: Thienhaus/Wippermann*
*Printed in Germany*

# CONTENTS

# Discover Barbados!

*This tropical island once lived from sugar;*
*nowadays, white beaches, outstanding hotels,*
*easy-going people and Caribbean flair lure visitors*

The aroma of exotic tropical spices fills the evening air. From the embers of the small grills, orange-red flames shoot up once in a while; their warm reflections are seen in the pots and salad bowls. The able hands of the cook cut up the large fish into smaller, more manageable portions in no time, placing them on the hot grill. Then he turns to you and asks: 'Do you want dolphin or kingfish?' Before you answer, he already knows what the reaction of the tourist will be and, as he quickly flips the fish portions over, he adds: 'But I don't mean the flipper fish!' Over the years, he has learned that foreigners will refuse to eat 'dolphin', so he has to explain that when they say dolphin, Barbadians really mean a delicious high-sea fish related to tuna and not to the ocean-living mammal.

It's not been long that the sun quickly dropped below the horizon, and the stalls in the fish market of Oistins are waiting for the evening rush of customers. I take my large portion of grilled 'dolphin' and place it next to my salad, then look for the ever-

*Partly hidden among the palms,*
*a typical wooden chattel house*
*in Bathsheba*

present *hot pepper sauce*, which in Barbados (as well as in the other Caribbean islands) accompanies just about any meal; it's the tropical equivalent of ketchup. Carrying my meal, I look for a comfortable spot and find a place on a plain wooden bench. I almost forgot it, but the cook has already read my mind and soon he yells to his wife who is standing near the refrigerator: 'A Banks for the lady, please.' And it's true, virtually everyone accompanies a meal with the *Banks*, the local beer of Barbados.

On the other end of the square, by the ultra-modern fish market, the last fish are sold under the glaring neon lights. Much later, between midnight and four o'clock in the morning, when the fish vendors are fast asleep in their homes, all fish cooks will be busier than ever grilling one portion after another. After all, today is Friday, and the Bajans - the way the Barbadians prefer to call themselves - celebrate the beginning of the weekend. After one mouthful of fish and one, two, three or even four beers, they slowly make their way to the nightclubs of nearby St Lawrence Gap and of the capital city of Bridgetown. Others decide to stay where they are perhaps because quite a few friends will come over. No later than during the return trip, when after endless dancing and countless *jump ups* the stomach begins to rumble, it's once again time to rest in Oistins.

The Bajans have dressed up for the occasion; the men wear long pants and shirts, their hair is nicely cut. Some of them have the small, twisted Rasta-locks pointing to all four directions of the compass. The women wear tight miniskirts and short t-shirts showing their belly-buttons; their hair has been tamed into a multitude of shining, black mini-braids, a practice called *cornrowing*. They all gather in small groups and talk, even laugh. Girlfriends are seen holding hands, walking from one group to the next, giggling. From the nearby bar, the latest rhythms are heard, the latest hit of the season is played and instantly recognized; everybody starts singing the refrain, soon the legs and hips start moving and shaking.

Measuring only 34 km (20 miles) by 22 km (about 15 miles), rectangular-shaped Barbados is not precisely large. Nevertheless, it's the most densely populated island in the Caribbean. Approximately 260,000 Bajans live on this tiny fleck of land, a little out of the way from the other islands of the lesser Antilles, better known as the Windward Islands. The constant trade winds blow incessantly, making the tropical climate bearable. The average daytime temperature oscillates between 28° and 31°C (80° and 88°F); in the evenings, the temperature seldom falls under 21°C (70°F). Brief, but heavy showers occur throughout the year, less so during the drier winter and early spring. Most of the heavy precipitation falls from July until November, when the danger of a hurricane hitting the small island (and many others) is real. Luckily, the sunniest and safest months coincide with the European and North American winter months, making Barbados the ideal holiday destination.

In spite of its high population density, the island doesn't look overcrowded; there are no high-rise buildings and once the metropolitan area of Bridgetown has been left behind, traffic flows very well. On some remote country roads it's even possible not to see an oncoming vehicle for quite a while. More than one-half of the Bajans live in the southern part of the island, where the two large tourist centres are also found. This iswherethe famous powdery-white beaches are, as well as a large selection of accommodations to fit every pocketbook, countless restaurants and the lively nightlife.

In the lee of the island, the long stretch of white sand continues. The west coast is characterized by the typical, lush tropical vegetation of graceful palm trees and exotic flowers – huge, colourful poinsettias and bougainvilleas are everywhere, the inhabitants take their presence for granted. This is the most popular part of the island, where the elegant and beautiful hotels for the tourists as well as the exclusive villas of the rich and famous are. A couple of Hollywood stars find relaxation and privacy behind the high walls. Here, the palms seem to make a bow towards the bright blue waters of the Caribbean – one great postcard view after another.

The placid, transparent and turquoise waters of the Caribbean entice everyone to jump in and

*The steel band plays hot calypso rhythms on oil barrels*

swim, dive or engage in any other kind of water sports activity. And no wonder, with year-round water temperatures oscillating between pleasant 25°C (74°F) and warm 28°C (80°F) – you can swim every single day of the year. These ideal water temperatures also create the right conditions for corals to grow profusely, especially here on the west coast.

Indeed, the island of Barbados owes its very existence to the corals. Not long ago, geologically speaking, 600,000 years to be exact, the island slowly rose from the ocean. Unlike the great majority of its much older island neighbours, which are of volcanic origin, Barbados is made up entirely of coral limestone. This explains the relative flatness of the land, as well as the good drinking water. The porous limestone allows rainwater to seep in easily, creating a multitude of underground streams and caves.

Whereas the south and north are almost as flat as a board, the interior is covered by low hills; in the east near Bathsheba they reach all the way to the coast. Here is the wilder part of the island. The large, powerful waves of the Atlantic reach the east coast after travelling for many hundreds of miles of open ocean. When they finally meet land, the waves leave their energy in the strong surf of the white, sandy beach.

The island's highest elevation is 340-m-high Mount Hillaby, found in the edge of the hilly chain called the Scotland Districts in the northeast corner of the island. As opposed to the other parts, there are many different kinds of rocks here that have partly been uplifted by ancient faults. This region is clearly the oldest and most interesting from the geologic point of view: the hills are mostly bare, covered only by grass and low bushes here and there, giving the visitor the eerie feeling of being in Scotland. Only the temperatures remind you of being in the tropics; in the greener valleys, mango trees grow in profusion.

That Barbados is a coral island after all is proven by the island's edges. The gorgeous beaches with a combined length of 110 km are made of fine coral sand. Long ago, the inhabitants of the island learned how to build with durable material: plantation houses, churches and even some hotels are built from the pale gray stone. While the well-to-do always preferred to build their houses with the more expensive stone, the great majority of the population lived in small, wooden houses called *chattel houses,* which are seen everywhere in all shapes and colours. This type of construction originated in colonial times, when the slaves were allowed to build their own houses, although the land they built them on was not theirs. So, the word for movable property, *chattel,* was given to the houses, which very often were built on a foundation of loose stones.

Although all these houses follow the same basic plan, nevertheless they all look different, as every owner wants to give its property some individuality. This is best achieved through the creative use of colour: there are brown-, cream-, peach- or beige-coloured houses – and countless other combinations, but these are the favourite colours – all over the island. To stress individuality, the owners then paint their blinds, window frames, gables and the like with strong, contrasting colours. Soon, you'll look for and find 'your' favourite house and colour combination, soon to be replaced by yet another one. Owing to the humid, salty breeze, the houses have to be re-painted after only a few years, providing their owners with unlimited creative opportunities.

Most of the Bajans are the descendants of slaves imported from West Africa three centuries ago. The diminishing white minority descends from the former British colonial masters who built and ran the sugar cane plantations. Barbados is unique among all the other Lesser Antilles in that it was ruled by only one colonial power. Since the island achieved its independence in 1966, it chose to remain an independent member of the British Commonwealth of Nations, so its official head of state is Queen Elizabeth II, who is represented by the *Governor General.* So, British English is learned in schools, people drive on the left, and typically British courtesy is the rule. The administrative and educational institutions are modeled after their British counterparts, and the Anglican Church is the island's most important denomination. In the supermarkets, countless tins of corned beef are offered for sale – Barbados, a truly exotic Caribbean combination, is *very British, but also very African.*

Nowadays, the island's main industry is tourism. In order to protect its biggest asset as much as possible – unspoiled natural tropical beauty – most of the hotels have only about one hundred rooms, many a lot less and only two considerably more. Every effort has been made to adapt the architecture to the surroundings, huge concrete rows of impersonal hotels have been avoided.

Restaurants and lobbies are largely open and have few walls, so that the breeze can supply most of the cooling. Does a *candlelight dinner* in a warm Caribbean evening with a view of the ocean sound attractive? You have come to the right place, Barbados has a large selection of first-rate restaurants in the best locations offering delicious meals and good service.

Apart from tourism, agriculture still has economic importance. For many centuries, Barbados was one more 'sugar island', the cultivation of sugar cane made the colonial masters wealthy. In the interior, sugar cane plantations still characterize the landscape. A sea of tall, pale green giant grasses rustle in the tropical breeze; the gentle green waves move endlessly into the horizon. Here and there, the monotonous landscape is interrupted by a palm tree or the stumps of old sugar mills. After 16 months, the cane is as tall as a human being and ready to be harvested. Just before the harvest starts, in November, when the sap

*Bottom Bay in the south-east coast: white sand, palm trees and turquoise water*

# History at a glance

**1536**
Portugese seafarers accidentally discover the island while looking for Brazil and gave it the name of 'Os Barbados', which means the 'bearded ones', because the numerous fig trees with their hanging air roots reminded them of long beards

**1627**
Two years after the island was taken by the British trader John Powell, the first colonizers land in Holetown to settle the island

**1637**
Sugar cane is first imported and cultivated

**1639**
Creation of the first Parliament, the British Commonwealth's third-oldest

**1831**
The emancipated blacks obtain the right to vote

**1838**
The British Parliament announces the abolition of slavery for all colonies in 1834. Soon thereafter, in 1840, the former slaves become citizens with full rights

**1924**
The Democratic League, the first black political coalition, is created

**1938**
The Social Democratic Barbados Labour Party (BLP) is formed

**1950**
The first representative, elected government takes office after the introduction of the right to vote

**1966**
The former British crown colony becomes independent on 30 November, but remains within the British Commonwealth of Nations. The first prime minister is Errol Barrow

**1971**
The liberal Democratic Labour Party (DLP) wins the elections by a margin of two-thirds

**1976**
The BLP regains power with Tom Adams thanks to a two-third majority. He wins the next elections in 1981 as well

**1986**
The DLP wins with a landslide, Earl Barrow becomes prime minister again

**1994**
After a no-confidence vote, the BLP wins in the early elections

**1999**
The BLP under prime minister Owen Arthur wins by a wide margin

or juice in the stems is sweet enough, many of the ordinarily respectable Bajans sneak into the fields to nibble a sweet treat at a 'sugar pole'.

Until recent years, from February to May the cane had to be patiently beaten by hand in order to get out the sweet, precious liquid; luckily, more and more machines are seen taking over this dull, back-breaking work. This is when wagonloads of sugar cane move towards the sugar refinery. There are three large ones, but twenty years ago, there were more than forty operating. In their vicinity, the characteristic, sweet and heavy smell of sugar being refined pervades the air. At the end of many complicated processes, the sweet, golden-white crystals, the source of so much wealth, leave the refinery packed in small bags, ready to be exported to all corners of the world. Some parts of the cane remain, though: the squeezed-out left-overs are sent back to the fields to be used as fertilizer, and molasses, the thick dark brown mass, goes to the rum factories to manufacture and export world-famous Barbados rum – but a lot stays and is drunk on the island.

The small pub on the corner is a local Barbadian institution; inside these *rum shops* the vast majority of the customers are male. It's pointless to try to count these shops; every little village, as small and insignificant as it may be, will have its local *rum shop* as well as its village church! Going to church is a deeply rooted custom, too. All Bajans, and not only the women, go to church often and enthusiastically; Sunday service is the high point of the week, and it doesn't matter to which one of the 140 religious denominations the people belong to.

But Sunday is not only the day of worship, prayer and singing. Barbadians love picnics, and whole extended families are often seen driving out to their favourite picnic grounds, the best ones being by the shore. Bajans love to swim and frolic in the water. After a good swim, the food and the cold beverages taste twice as good. To accompany the meal, radio-cassettes playing the latest tunes are as much a part of the landscape as palms and sand. Calypso lets the hearts beat faster and livens things up; soon everybody starts swinging and the picnic has turned into a spontaneous little party. In late July and early August, it's an *all day party* when the sugar harvest is over. Then, people celebrate for weeks, culminating on *Kandooment Day*, when the island's largest costume party takes place. Then, it's non-stop dancing on the whole island.

The charm of Barbados lies not only in the numerous, idyllic beaches, the comfortable hotels, the good restaurants, the solid infrastructure and the low crime, what makes this little island so special are its people, the Bajans, who with their friendliness and their willingness to help every visitor who comes to this Caribbean jewel, allow everyone to partake in their positive outlook on life. They have managed to achieve a certain level of prosperity in their thirty-odd years of independence, and their educational level is higher than in most of the other Caribbean islands. Quite understandably, they are proud of their achievements.

# Calypso and green monkeys

*A few facts are needed
to understand the Bajans a little better*

### Grantley Adams

Sir Grantley Adams (1898-1971) became the first prime minister of Barbados in 1954 and he was also the head of the now defunct *Federation of the West Indies* during its short-lived existence. A member of Parliament since 1934, the lawyer and linguist became the leader of the *Barbados Labour Party* (BLP) in 1939, one year after its founding. He was one of the founding fathers of the Federation and after its demise he was one of the main architects of Barbadian independence, working intensively to change the status of his home country from British Crown Colony to independent state.

His son J. M. G. M. (Tom) Adams followed in the footsteps of his famous father, leading the BLP to victory in 1976. He was the country's Prime Minister until his sudden death in 1984.

### Aloe vera

This large plant looks like it has thick meaty leaves, but in reality they are stems. As a member of the succulent family, it saves water by

*A Rastafarian weaving a basket*

having thorny leaves and storing the precious liquid in the green stems). Brought from the Mediterranean countries by the white settlers, the plant adapted quickly to the new environment. Its curative properties are held in high esteem by the islanders; the leaves contain a gel-like substance with healing powers which is also used as an ingredient for cosmetics. The gel is especially good for restoring the health of sunburned skin and combating skin infections. It can be bought everywhere on the island, on the beach (too expensive) or in the supermarket (reasonably priced).

Aloe vera has an extremely bitter taste and has been used by Bajan mothers for decades as a means of discouraging their children from sucking their thumbs. No wonder many adult Bajans have unpleasant childhood memories!

### Errol Barrow

The political opponent of Sir Grantley Adams, Errol Barrow (1920-1987), grew up partly in the USA, where he studied economics. Returning to his native Barbados in 1950, he helped to found the *Democratic Labour Party* (DLP), becoming prime minister of Barbados in 1961 after his party swept him into power. In 1966, he was confirmed as the independent nation's first prime minister. He stayed in the job until 1976. After the DLP won the elections once more in 1986, he returned to his post and remained Prime Minister until his sudden death in 1987.

## Population

For the most part, Bajans are the direct descendants of African slaves brought from West Africa. Between 1640 and 1804, approx. 387,000 Africans were taken to this little island, to be subsequently shipped to other islands as well as to North America. As opposed to other Caribbean islands, African influence soon waned; in 1817 only seven per cent of the slaves had been born in the Dark Continent, whereas in Jamaica this percentage was as high as 36 and in Trinidad even 44 per cent. For this reason, an African cult like voodoo is completely unknown here. Nevertheless, African culture influence is pervasive and is kept alive. For example, it can be seen in the *tuk bands,* in the large number of African sayings or in dishes like *coucou.*

Approximately 260,500 Bajans live in Barbados, more than 55 per cent in the southern part of the island, in the communities of St Michael (which includes the capital of Bridgetown) and Christ Church. Almost 93 per cent of the population is black, approximately four per cent are mulatto and three per cent white. The remaining are a combination of races.

## Education

Since independence was achieved in 1966, the government has invested heavily in education, spending more than 20 per cent of the nation's revenue on it, a very high proportion for Caribbean and even First World standards. Since schooling is mandatory for anyone under 16, more than 97 per cent of the population can read and write. The educational system includes primary and secondary schools. Formal school education ends with a diploma. Apart from state schools, there are a number of renowned private schools as well as a technical college specializing in hotel management. The well-known University of the West Indies has several faculties.

## Calypso

Barbados swings to calypso tunes. Apart from Trinidad, this island is the stronghold of this music whose origins can be traced back to West African rhythms. Calypso became famous in Europe and North America as early as the 1950's owing mostly to Harry Belafonte's hit 'Banana boat'. Since then, calypso has remained a very popular rhythm because it also it expresses the political opinion of the masses with its heavy dosage of satire, mockery and gossip. Every year, during the traditional *Crop Over Festival,* the *King of Calypso* is chosen – a national event.

It is danced in a very original way. Both dancing partners stand behind one another, the woman in front of the man. The hips start to move in a circle until they find the rhythm, then the torso starts moving. Soon, the music animates the crowd; long lines of dancers come to the dance floor. This is not at all improper, but seen as something completely normal. On the other hand, pairs of lovers smooching are rarely seen.

*Soca* is another kind of calypso, but in contrast to the 'pure' calypso, it has fewer political and social connotations having even more rhythm instead. For some, this is the disco variant of calypso. Soca came into being only since the 1970's.

Just as popular are steel bands. In the hotels, apart from the ever-popular calypso tunes, international hits are played on oil drums converted to musical instruments.

## Chattel house

The story of the small, colourful wooden houses seen everywhere on the island is an interesting one. After the slaves were emancipated in 1838, most of the land was still in the hands of the planters. Soon thereafter, in 1840, the free blacks were allowed to build their own homes and pay a low rent as long as they built them in the less productive parts of the island. The plantation owners nevertheless retained the right to evict troublesome occupants on short notice from their lands. For this reason, the houses had to be moveable properties, ready to be taken apart in a single day. Back then, their parts were transported in an ox-cart, nowadays tractors are used for the same purpose.

The façade is always symmetrical; the door in the middle is flanked by the two windows. The size of the house and its decoration faithfully reflect the financial position of the occupant. The core of the house consists of one unit containing two rooms under a gable roof; the second (and in some cases, a third) element is formed by one or more rooms,

each one having its separate roof. So very often, one sees two pointed roofs beside or behind one another and in addition, a shed with a flat roof, where the kitchen usually is. The houses rest on loose, piled-up stones; the traditional wooden shingle roof has been mostly replaced by a corrugated-iron roof.

Lately, the *chattel house* is not the one and only place of residence any longer; nevertheless, the owners still take good and loving care of them. When they pass away, some of them are converted to boutiques. Sometimes, whole villages made of *chattel houses* are created for the benefit of tourists.

## Fauna

Barbados is not exactly an animal paradise where countless different animal species are found. Apart from the numerous pets brought by the early settlers, the green African monkeys have established themselves well. Other imported animals are the mungos (marten-like viverrids) introduced to control the endemic snakes. Sadly, nowadays the reptiles have been driven to extinction, whereas the mungos are plentiful. The island has some local species of lizards as well as bats and 24 species of birds. Another 18 species use the island as a resting stop in the winter. The bird species have diminished, too. Some of the most common ones are: the *black-birds* (Quiscalus lugubris), *wood doves* (Zenai-da aurita), sparrows (Loxigilla noctis), *yellow breasts* (Coereba flaveola) and the *doctor boobies*. On the shore, frigate birds are often seen, although they are not endemic to the island. Herons like to be in cultivated

*Be careful! A caustic sap from the manchineel tree drops down after a shower*

fields, especially on sugar cane plantations.

There is only one endemic species of frog, the brown, two-centimetre-(approximately one-inch)-long *whistling frog*. In the evenings, one hears their sound resembling the word 'coqui', sung in duet with the chirping crickets.

## Flora

Although it boasts about 700 different flower species, it nevertheless cannot be said that Barbadian flora is plentiful when compared to that found on other Caribbean islands. Still, that's a lot. Particularly beautiful and exotic are some of the tree species, like the bearded *fig tree* (Ficus citrifolia). Although not as plentiful as it once was when the Portuguese named the little island after this impressive tree with its huge, hanging aerial roots, it can still be seen in and around some villages. The best ones grow in Welchman Hall Gully, around Codrington College and in the Andromeda Gardens.

Palms are as part of a Caribbean island as the bright sun and beautiful beaches. Apart from the common coconut and king palm, the similar *cabbage palm* is seen almost everywhere. The palm crown can reach a height of almost 40 m, which is 10 metres more than the normally 30-m-high king palms. These beautiful tropical trees can be best appreciated in the imposing palm boulevard opposite Codrington College.

Very common on the beaches are the species of *Casuarina*, also known as the *mile tree* and *manchineel*. Whereas the former has needle-shaped leaves which are completely harmless, the manchineel should best be seen from afar. Its small, green and round fruit is extremely poisonous and the tree produces a white sap that is highly caustic and can easily injure the skin.

Mahogany trees were introduced approximately 250 years ago, and some of the best furniture in the plantation homes was made from this priceless wood. Nowadays, their numbers have dwindled, but there is still an impressive mahogany boulevard in Cherry Tree Hill.

The strange-looking tree with the very fragrant blossoms is the *frangipani* (Plumeria rubra). It is not very high and the branches are widely spaced; in the dry season it gets rid of its leaves to conserve water. What makes frangipanis some of the favourite little trees of the tropics are their beautiful orange-red, pink and white blossoms. The other favourite is the poinciana or flame of the forest, better known on the island as the *flamboyant*. This tree waits until the moist summer months to bring out its huge orange-red blossoms. During the dry winter months, the tree is bare and the long, dark pods hang listlessly from the branches. Another one is the *silk cotton* having massive board-like roots; its fruit is made of a cotton-like substance which gave this tree its name. Lining the streets one often sees the large breadfruit trees with their characteristic large, dark green leaves.

Perhaps the most important of the local fruit trees is the *Barbados cherry*. Its fruits resemble its Northern European counterparts but are rather tart, so they are best eaten cooked or as marmalade. They have a high vitamin C content and are therefore used by the beverage industry.

## Flying Fish

This unusual fish is quite common throughout the Caribbean, but it's only in Barbados where it's caught and eaten. It is not solitary, preferring to live in large schools. Fishermen catch it from December to June with their nets. This remarkable fish can remain out of the water for more than 20 seconds and glide with a top speed of 55 km/h. To achieve this feat, it uses its tail fin as a propeller and the other four fins as sails so it can glide like a plane!

## Geography and geology

Barbados is the easternmost of the Caribbean islands and lies only 13 degrees north of the equator. Geographically speaking, it's part of the Lesser Antilles, and it is a small island indeed: only 34 km long and a maximum width of 22.5 km. Its area of 431 square kilometres makes it about as big as Manchester and Liverpool combined.

The oldest parts of the island emerged from the ocean only 600,000 years ago, which makes this island of coral origin the youngest of the Lesser Antilles, which are volcanic and have emerged almost 50 million years ago. The coral limestone layer has an average thickness of 65 m and covers about 85 per cent of the island.

Under the ground, the island resembles Swiss cheese: rainwater rapidly percolates through the porous limestone, where it collects in underground streams, ponds and caves. Only in the Scotland District, where the limestone layer has eroded away, is it possible to see what was once the ocean floor.

## Colonial times

Columbus either didn't see the island or was indifferent to it. It got its name from the Portuguese who sailed by. The first white men who set foot on the island, however, were the British in 1625. Only two years later, they came to settle the largely uninhabited place. The colony barely grew at first; it was composed of a curious mix of adventurers, outcasts and political refugees who sought a new beginning in the New World.

In the 1640's, the cultivation of sugar cane began. Soon, large areas were planted with the sweet grass and the colony was able to ship substantial quantities of sugar to the mother country. An economic boom set in, so more people were needed for the back-breaking work, and soon enough the infamous slave trade began. This industry flourished as well, and became very well organized. In the ensuing years, a good part of the original forest disappeared to make room for the sugar plantations. As opposed to other islands fleeing slaves could hardly find hiding places in the predominantly flat, open island and the next island was 150 km away! Sooner or later, the slaves revolted more than once, but they were mercilessly put down.

The 18th century brought about some changes. So, for example, the half-caste children from whites and blacks were given some freedom, and last but not least the French Revolution had important repercussions even here, where for the first time human rights were mentioned. Slowly but surely, a society based on the slave trade began tottering. In 1807, Britain decided to end the slave trade, but it was only in 1834 that all slaves were nominally set free. Four more years had to elapse until they really gained their freedom. Until then, blacks had to complete a sort of 'training period' for their former

masters. Only afterwards could they leave the property. The planters made the transition difficult by enacting special laws. In the end, the former slaves had to work just as hard as in the past, the only difference was that to compensate for their hard work, they could lease a tiny plot of land from their employers. In case of dismissal, they lost their homes. The system worked, and the economy boomed again until many blacks left the island to work for higher wages in the building of the Panama Canal, sending their hard-earned money to support their families back home. When they finally returned, they had enough cash to buy a real plot of land. Another factor that helped them to achieve that goal was the fall of the sugar price, which forced many plantation owners to sell cheaply.

In the 1920's, Marcus Garvey, a black Jamaican, called upon all blacks to end white oppression, and black political and social self-consciousness was born. Three-day riots in 1937 finally forced substantial political changes leading to the creation of the Barbados Labour Party (BLP) the following year. Its leader Grantley Adams campaigned for the rights of Barbadian workers. Yet Barbados had to wait until 1966 to become a fully independent nation after the collapse of the West Indian Federation with Trinidad/Tobago and Jamaica in 1962.

## Cricket

This sport originated in England in the 16th century and is one of the most popular ones played in the British Commonwealth. The

*West Indies* have some of the very best teams. The islands of Jamaica, Trinidad and Barbados always produce legendary players, such as the Barbadian Frank Worrel, who was knighted by the Queen in 1964. He can be seen in all five-dollar notes.

Cricket is a ball game played by two opposing teams of eleven players each, who are either batters or catchers. The batting team is made up of two batsmen standing in front of the cricket goals and an additional nine cricket players who relieve the two batsmen. The catching team consist of a bowler, a goalkeeper and nine field players. The batting team takes on the defence of the goals. They are the only ones who can score. The *batsman* tries to strike the ball thrown to his area as far away into the other side as possible so he can change places as much as possible with the batsman. Every *run* means one point. The *bowler* of the batting team may throw up to six balls into the goal of the opposing team, then he is relieved. The catcher behind the goal and the nine field players try to 'knock out' the batsmen of the opposing team throwing the balls towards the goal. One round is over when ten *batsmen* are knocked out, then it's the other team's turn.

The most important national cricket tournaments take place between January and April, and they are very prominent events lasting several days. The cricket clubs organize their tournaments in the remaining months.

### Agriculture
In the past, the traditional agricultural exports were tobacco, cotton and sugar cane. Currently,

*Another African immigrant: the Barbados green monkey*

cotton and sugar are still important exports, but cut flowers, cherries, papayas and other tropical fruits have been added to the list: bananas, breadfruit, citrus, mangos, maize, yams, sweet potatoes, *sweet* and *hot peppers* and other seasonal fruits and vegetables. However, with increasing tourism, the importance of agriculture has decreased. This is especially seen in the dwindling of the sugar cane fields; with every passing year, less and less is devoted to its cultivation.

### Green monkeys
Zoologically speaking, these Old World monkeys introduced to Barbados 350 years ago have thrived. The green monkeys (Cercopithecus aethiops sabaeus) came with the slave traders to the New World and zoologists can tell whether a certain monkey is from Barbados or Africa, its origi-

nal home. For example, the New World cousin has more dog-like features, making them a sub-species officially baptized by zoologists as the Barbados green monkey. Approximately 5,000 to 8,000 of the animals live on the island, usually in groups of 15 led by a dominant, or 'alpha-male'. They love to loot cultivated fields and gardens and as a result of the plentiful food available, their numbers are often out of control. Farmers, ruined and angry by the damage done to their crops, have created a self-help organization called *Monkey Damage Crop Control,* in order to put a stop to their exploding population.

If you are lucky, you will see the comical monkeys; some of the best places are in Welchman Hall Gully and in the Barbados Wildlife Refuge (where you by all means will see them).

## Politics

The island's first Parliament was set up as early as 1639 and it is the third-oldest in the English-speaking world. Barely six years later, in 1645, Barbados was subdivided into eleven *parishes*, which still exist today. They are: St Michael, Christ Church, St Philip, St John, St George, St Joseph, St Andrew, St Peter, St Lucy, St James and St Thomas.

For several centuries, the right to vote was reserved for those privileged few who owned land. It was only until 1831 that all citizens, including blacks, got the right to vote in elections.

The first modern political party was founded in 1938, the Barbados Labour Party (BLP). It dominated the political scene until 1961, and its long-time leader

was Grantley (later Sir) Adams. Independence from Great Britain finally became a reality on 30 November 1966 with Prime Minister Errol Walton Barrow of the Democratic Labour Party (DLP), the rival party formed in 1955. As a member of the Commonwealth, Queen Elizabeth II is still the Barbadian head of state. She is represented on the island by the governor-general, Sir Hugh Springer. The island's Parliament is made up of representatives elected from the Upper House (the local equivalent of the House of Lords) every five years. In 1976 and 1981, the BLP was able to gain the majority of the votes; in 1986 Barrow returned to power. In 1994, his party was once again replaced by the BLP under Owen Arthur, who was re-elected in 1999.

## Religion

By and large, Bajans are Anglican, but there are more than 100 other denominations and religious sects on the little island, the most important ones being the Methodists, Catholics, *Pentecostals*, Seventh Day Adventists and spiritual Baptists who are recognized by their colourful robes and scarves. They are better known by their name *tie-heads*.

One of the last spiritual movements to reach and gain an important foothold on the island has been the Rastafarian movement from Jamaica, arriving in 1975. The Rastafarians believe that Haile Selassie, the former Emperor of Ethiopia was the direct descendant of King David and King Solomon and they worship him as Jah, their God. They can be easily recognized by their long and uncombed strands of hair called *dreadlocks*. Their influence has been important as they have contributed to a strengthening of black self-awareness not only in Barbados or Jamaica, but throughout the West Indies. Rastafarians are mostly vegetarian, are teetotalers and instead of smoking tobacco they smoke marihuana, which they call *ganja*. Its smoking is strictly prohibited in Barbados, though. They work especially as artisans and artists; many are also street vendors who offer tasty snacks. Others sell herbal extracts with healing powers or live more isolated as farmers.

## Language

The official language is English, but most of the inhabitants speak a Creole dialect, which might be a little difficult to understand at first. Bear in mind, however, that it is sometimes as hard for Bajans to understand our English as it is for us to understand theirs! To please you, many will make great efforts to speak correct English. To help you out a little bit, the following differences to Oxford English should be remembered: 'th' is pronounced as 't' or 'd'; thus, the number 'three' sounds more like 'tree' and 'them' like 'dem'. Compared to other English-speaking islands in the Lesser Antilles, the vocabulary of Barbadians has relatively few words of African origin. Some of them are: *warri*, a board game, *coucou*, a dish, and *okra*, a vegetable the slaves brought from their native Africa.

## Natives

The original inhabitants of the island were the Arawak and Carib Indians, who after fighting one another, had left the island even before the arrival of the white settlers in 1627. Archaeologists have found few remains of their presence on the island.

## Industry and trade

Tourism has replaced agriculture as the country's number one industry. More than 12,000 beds in approximately 140 hotels belonging to all categories, plus the countless cruise ships anchoring in Bridgetown provide employment to 20,000 Barbadians. Agriculture still means mostly the production of sugar cane and derivatives, such as rum. However, tourism has brought some diversification in the agricultural industry, so that lately there has been an increased cultivation of fruits and vegetables as well as more production of meat and poultry. Cotton remains an important crop. Another important industry is fishing with its two centres of Bridgetown and Oistins. The most important fish are the *dolphin* and the *flying fish*.

Barbados is one of only four Caribbean islands that have the good fortune of relying partly on their own oil fields to meet part of their energy demand – in the case of Barbados, one-third of it. Other industries are clothing, furniture, the assembly of electronic parts and medical articles. Also important as a source of income are the so-called *offshore services* for foreign companies. Overall, Barbados is a prosperous country by Caribbean standards. In spite of the progress achieved in the last decades and of the relatively high level of education, more than 20 per cent of the population is unable to find a job.

# Brunch, Bajanian style

*Flying fish and stuffed chicken accompanied by macaroni soufflé or fried plantains and for dessert, a slice of coconut cake*

Fish and meat, as well as generously portioned side-dishes are the main courses of every banquet. It therefore comes as no surprise that every time Bajanian specialities are announced, the customer expects large buffets, be it in the hotel restaurant, the folkloric event or the Sunday brunch in the holiday resort.

Fried chicken and *flying fish* are the most popular dishes and will be found in every buffet. If they are stuffed with herbs, they'll taste even better. With a little bit of luck, you may have the opportunity of trying the famous *pepperpot*. In this kind of stew, several different kinds of meat go into the pot. And everybody will tell you that the more often it is re-heated, the better it will taste. To accompany the hearty stew, you may get *fried plantains*, *fried breadfruit* (the Caribbean variant of chips), *pickled breadfruit*, baked and candied sweet potatoes (somewhat mealier and sweeter than their European counterparts) or *pumpkin fritters*. The so-called classical side-dishes of rice,

*Able hands quickly prepare tasty fish*

macaroni soufflé and potato salad can also be ordered as well.

*Cakes* are delicacies that are offered in cocktail receptions, but in this case they are not what everybody expects, but deep-fried little balls. If they are made with fish, Bajans call them *fish cakes*, if spinach is added instead, then they are known as *spinach cakes* etc. To make them taste better, a few drops of sweet-sour, hot or remoulade sauce should be added. To round up a generous meal, sweet cakes are ideal desserts, and Bajans know how to bake them, whether they are made of cheese or coconut.

Not everyone gets excited about *pudding and souse*, a hearty Sunday meal that is fixed either by the housewife or can be bought in the markets. The pudding is made of sweet potatoes that are then put in sausage skin and steamed. They are usually eaten with pickled and marinated sour pork, which may include the heads and feet, too.

Those who love the taste of fresh fish have come to the right place. By all means, don't miss the Oistins Fishmarket, where you can eat not only the best fresh fish on the island, but a large va-

*The Oistins Fish Market: hot fish fillets from the charcoal grill served all night long*

riety of other foods as well. Every evening, the fish fillets are placed on the hot charcoal grills and eaten as soon as they land on the plate – a delicious and very reasonably priced supper. It is also possible to get them in front of the clubs in St Lawrence Gap.

In Barbados, fish is plentiful, which is explained by the island's proximity to the deep waters of the Atlantic, so the fishermen can catch deep-water fish in their nets more easily than the other Caribbean islanders. What makes Barbadians unique is their love for flying fish. Only in Barbados it is caught and eaten in such large proportions. After all, the island's national dish is *flying fish* with *coucou,* a porridge resembling mashed potatoes made of maize flour and okra, a vegetable the slaves brought from Africa. The best coucou needs the culinary skills of a Bajan housewife, which is the reason it's seldom seen on menus. On the other hand, fried flying fish can be had almost everywhere, either as a sandwich or by itself, always with a shot of fiery *hot pepper sauce.* It's the ideal and nutritious mid-afternoon snack. Other

recommended fish are the *dolphin* and the *kingfish,* both of them tasty deep-sea fish.

Why don't you try fish prepared the *blackened* way? The meat is cut in strips and marinated with herbs, then fried. Two other delicious fish found in the menus of restaurants are *red snapper* and *marlin.* Don't forget to ask for the daily special! *Lobster* and *crab* are also served fresh, but they are not from Barbados' shores; they are caught in the neighbouring Grenadines.

The Bajans don't eat out very often unless it's a special occasion. Instead, they prefer picnics, a Sunday institution to which they bring many different dishes. Sometimes, people meet for lunch or brunch in one of the many brunch-buffets. Those who work in the city may meet a colleague for a noon chat while enjoying lunch. For those on the go, a *roti,* a stuffed round piece of dough that originated in India, might be a better idea. Last but not least, fast food can also be found here, although hamburgers are not especially popular. So, for example, the world's largest fast food chain had to close its outlets after finding out that Bajans have little sympa-

24

thy for the round beef patties. *Chefette*, a local company, has the most outlets. If you are just looking for plain but good Bajan fare accompanied by a nice salad buffet, then you have come to the right location.

There is a very good selection of restaurants offering all kinds of tempting dishes. If you are just a little hungry, the bars by the beach are your best option. They offer true Caribbean flair and serve tasty sandwiches, pizza, salads etc. plus the ever-present but good flying fish. They are truly the best places for those who love informality and don't feel like following stiff *dress codes* and would rather keep their shorts on in the evening. The beach bars are also the ideal places for treating yourself to a *sundowner*: *Happy Hour* are the two magic words that act like magnets and fill the bars. Incidentally: those bars situated in St Lawrence Gap are most likely to have not only one, but even two and sometimes three Happy Hours. The first one is late in the morning, the second one at the usual time of the day right before sunset and the third one is for those who want to sample the local nightlife, between dinnertime and 11 pm.

As small as the island is, the culinary selection is nevertheless astounding: Italian, Austrian, Mexican and a potpourri of the very best of several national dishes. Best of all: every dish is prepared with fresh ingredients, nothing is frozen. The upper end of the scale is presently marked by the *Cliff* (in *Derricks, St James*). This is where perfection rules: the dishes, the service, the atmosphere. Yet there are so many other good restaurants serving delicious food directly on the beach that a short holiday will never give you enough time to sample all their delicious and unforgettable dishes.

In addition to the well-known international drinks that are served in every bar and hotel, there are a couple of highly recommended drinks. One of them is the local beer called *Banks*, an outstanding brew and much more reasonably priced than its imported counterparts. You may also want to sample the good *Red Stripe* from Jamaica as well as the *Carib* from neighbouring Trinidad.

The classical cocktail in this rum island is *rum punch*. It has the colour of a setting sun and tastes sweet but is not sticky and has a spicy aftertaste – at least this is the way it should taste. Why don't you sample several ones prepared in different places? You will soon find out that there are significant differences in the quality. The connoisseurs prefer the creamy variant of the rum liqueur *Crisma*, which reminds you of Baileys and can likewise be drunk with ice. Another very typical local drink is the liqueur called *Falernum*, made from sugar cane. Mixed with lemon juice and sugar, it is the main ingredient of many other cocktails.

And then there's rum, of course. It comes in many different presentations and qualities. The older it is, the smoother the taste on your tongue. Other countries have wine cellars, but here in Barbados, the places to go are the *rum shops*, where some of the best rum you will ever try can be tasted in an original setting – and the Bajans will be delighted to be your hosts.

# Cool drinks out of clay monkeys

*Pottery has been a tradition for almost two hundred years,
now it is a very popular and traditional souvenir*

The production of pottery has had a long tradition in Barbados. It all started with the production of containers for the sugar industry, when jugs for collecting molasses resulting from the sugar refining process were needed. The female slaves were the ones who in the 19th century started making the clay jugs, and soon thereafter they made numerous other pottery pieces. An important pottery centre was and still is *Chalky Mount* located in the Scotland District. The pottery produced there has simple patterns, the best known container being the so-called *monkey*, a sealable water jug with a pointed snout and a large handle. The appropriately named pottery production centre called *Earthworks* in the western part of the island created more modern and daring colours and patterns.

The Rastafarians have specialized in carvings, jewellery and leather. Their products can be seen and purchased in the *Rasta Market* in Bridgetown or in fairs. Another good place with a wide selection of handcrafts is *Pelican Village*, near the harbour and also in the *Chattel Vil-*

*lage* in Holetown. The shops of the souvenir chain *Best of Barbados* also sell interesting crafts, but you have to ignore all the other kitschy souvenirs. Among other things, this chain also has a good selection of informative nature guides and other books dealing with the flora and fauna, as well as about the island's history. The numerous *duty free shops* scattered throughout the Caribbean almost invariably offer the same items for sale, such as cosmetics, spirits, sunglasses and jewellery. Some art galleries sell the creations of local artists, and some of them can be attractive indeed. Typical motifs of some colourful canvases are depictions of the lush tropical vegetation growing around the *chattel house*.

On the beach, hawkers offer tourists beach towels, t-shirts, sunhats made of woven palm leaves, jewellery and many more things. Once back home, get out the hot red pepper sauce, a good bottle of rum and relax while you bring back the memories of tropical Barbados and the warm sea breeze.

Shops are open Mon–Fri 8 am–4 pm sometimes until 5 pm, Sat from 8 am–1 pm, large supermarkets until 9 pm or 10 pm. No shops are open on Sundays or holidays.

*Chalky Mount, a pottery centre*

# Jump up

*When Bajans celebrate, it's an all day affair. During the Crop Over Festival, all the islanders are on their feet, dancing and singing: 'Jump & Raise Up Yuh Hands'*

**W**hether it is a traditional festival like the Oistins Fish or the Crop Over Festival, or an important religious holiday like Christmas or Good Friday or perhaps a political day of remembrance – Bajans really know how to celebrate. In addition to the eleven official holidays (if they fall on a Sunday, then they are observed the next Monday), there are a series of festivals lasting several days or even weeks.

The unsurpassed high point in the island is the famous Crop Over Festival that takes place in July/August, when the end of the sugar harvest is celebrated with non-stop dancing and music-making; the whole island goes crazy during the colourful hustle and bustle.

But festivals are not the only occasions when Barbadians love to sing and dance. As a matter of fact, religious services are also good opportunities to express their love of life: the whole church is filled with cheerful melodies accompanied by the tambourines. In a way, every Sunday is a little holiday worth celebrating. Since the religious service

*All the island dances. The costume parade on Kadooment Day is the high point of the Crop Over Festival*

is the day's highpoint, the Bajans dress up for the occasion as if they were attending a party. The ladies wear high-heeled shoes with elegant dresses and wide-brimmed hats to protect their faces from the hot tropical sun while their daughters wear tulledresses with colourful hair-slides. The gentlemen and their sons don't want to be left behind and wear elegant, dark suits – with a tie, of course.

Reggae, soca and above all calypso provide the necessary atmosphere for every festivity – some of the songs become so popular that they even make it to the local hit parade. Every year new hits flood the island from neigbouring Trinidad, but now and then Barbadian artists are successful exporting a catchy tune or two. Soon, every pupil and every saleswoman is heard whistling the new hit. In the evenings, the DJ's in the clubs tirelessly play the new melody again and again, the audience can't get enough of it. All live bands start outdoing each other with their versions of the new songs. Thus, at the Congerline Carnival in April/May, a Caribbean version of the Polonaise is introduced; and at Crop Over, all hell breaks loose. Even those stiff spectators slowly give up their resistance and join the

**1** **Oistins Fish Festival**
On Easter, the Barbadians celebrate this festival where everything revolves around fish and fun (page 30)

**2** **Crop Over Festival**
A cheerful harvest festival with many parades culminating in the crowning of the King of Calypso (page 31)

dancing crowds, they just can't resist such cheerfulness, boisterousness and joy of living!

## OFFICIAL HOLIDAYS

1 January: *New Year's Day*
*Good Friday*
*Easter Monday*
28 April: *Heroes Day*
1 May: *Labour Day*
*Whit Monday*
1 August: *Emancipation Day*
1st Monday in August: *Kadooment Day* (highpoint of the Crop Over Festival)
30 November: *Independence Day*
25 December: *Christmas Day*
26 December: *Boxing Day*

## EVENTS

### January
During the famous *Jazz Festival*, several emerging jazz bands play their best repertoire one weekend long in several places, trying to outdo each other.

### February
17 February, the day when the first settlers came to Barbados in 1627, serves as the prelude for the weeklong (**102/A–B4**) *Holetown Festival*. The little village on the west coast becomes the stage for all kinds of concerts, performances, street parades and markets.

### March
World-class international opera stars are guests of honour during the *Holder's Opera Season*. Even Luciano Pavarotti has come here to sing.

### March/April
★ On Easter Weekend, the little town of (**107/F5**) Oistins celebrates the *Oistins Fish Festival*, where everything revolves around the fish. All of the island's fishermen participate in the numerous competitions. The fishermen show off their skills in catching, filleting and cutting up fish, and a colourful supporting programme provides additional entertainment: live guest performances of Barbadian stars, gospel concerts and a large street market showing a good selection of local handcrafts. Last but not least, delicious fish dishes are offered as well. The festival is a typical Barbadian affair that reaches its climax on Easter Monday.

### April/May
The other famous festival is the *Congerline Carneval*, where for two weeks, national and international guest stars of the soca and calypso

music world show off their talents in two different fairgrounds. In the morning of May 1, the long 'queue' composed of bands and groups of singing and dancing pedestrians follow the musicians as they walk down the streets of (**106/107**) Bridgetown.

## May/June

During the *Gospel Festival* on Whitsun, all important gospel groups of the USA, England and the Caribbean meet on the island.

## July/August

★ The *Crop Over Festival* is the undisputed king of all Barbadian festivals. From mid-July to early August, cultural events, music competitions, street festivals and parades take place, three full weeks of non-stop celebrating. 'Crop over', the end of the sugar cane harvest, was always a good reason to celebrate. The festival begins the moment that the last sugar cane is taken to the mill. The opening ceremony takes place in a different place every year; the festival's high-point is the first week in August. Then, during the *Pic-O-De-Crop* in the National Stadium, the island's Calypso King is chosen by the jury. In the *Bridgetown Market*, hundreds of decorated stands along the Princess Alice Highway offer a wide selection of arts and crafts as well as delicious appetizers, while the tunes of music bands outdoing each other are heard from every corner. On the evening before the festival, the *Cohobblopot* provides the right atmosphere with musical and theatrical performances. Then, on *Kadooment Day*, the first Monday in August, every one of the islanders are on their feet, either participating in the countless street parades or just merrily celebrating with the others. This joyful celebration of life ends with fireworks.

## November

On the *National Independence Festival of the Creative Arts*, Bajans of all ages and from all parts of the island show off their musical, singing, dancing, acting or poetic talents. The final performance takes place on the last day of November, Independence Day.

*The colourful street market during the Oistins Fish Festival on Easter*

# White beaches, wind, waves and nightlife

*The 'Riviera' of Barbados offers both relaxation and pleasure, whilst the capital city of Bridgetown pulsates with business*

The turquoise waters of the Caribbean shimmer along the shore, gradually changing their colour to deeper shades of blue as they recede towards the horizon, where

*The Parliament in Bridgetown*

they finally meet the sky. Heavy, puffy white clouds sail by, and surfers wait for the steady breeze to fill their colourful sails, allowing them to rush and jump over the waves. The beaches are padded with soft, powdery-white sand. Here and there, casuarinas wear-

---

### Hotel and restaurant prices

**Hotels**
*Category 1*: over 200 US$
*Category 2*: 80 to 200 US$
*Category 3*: to 80 US$
Prices are for two persons in one double room without breakfast in the high season (Dec.–April) if booked individually. In the low season, the prices can be as much as 50 per cent lower. Single rooms cost only a little less. Five per cent *government tax* has to be added; sometimes ten per cent is added as *service charge*, especially in the better hotels.

**Restaurants**
*Category 1*: from 45 Bds$
*Category 2*: 30 to 45 Bds$
*Category 3*: to 30 Bds$
Prices are for the main course excluding drinks and taxes.

**Important abbreviations**

| | |
|---|---|
| **Bds$** | Barbadian Dollar |
| **US$** | US Dollar |
| **Ave.** | Avenue |
| **Rd.** | Road |
| **Str.** | Street |

---

ing their light green dress made of needle-like leaves give a little shade, while the palm fans rustle in the Caribbean wind. Bright orange wooden towers with an observation platform on top keep watch over the lively bustle down on the beach.

Almost the whole southern coast is one long uninterrupted stretch of beach. The numerous, more or less circular bays and coves follow one another, yet each one has its own atmosphere. Miami Beach near Oistins, for example, is the favourite weekend meeting place for Bajans, while Sandy or Dover Beach is the preferred destination of the holiday-makers. West of the island's southernmost tip, the scenery changes and becomes wilder. Crane Beach and Bottom Bay are unspoiled beaches that revive the yearning for more freedom and adventure.

The southern coast, especially its western part, is highly populated. More than half of the island's population lives in the parishes of St Michael (pop. approx. 97,500), to which the capital city of Bridgetown belongs, and Christ Church (pop. approx. 47,000). The urban expansion continues farther into the south. Gradually, the traditional wooden *chattel houses* are being replaced or surrounded by small, detached one-family houses which prove that Barbadians have achieved a certain degree of modest prosperity. Extreme social disparities are less obvious in Barbados than in some other islands of the Caribbean.

The infrastructure in this part of the island is outstanding. From Sir Grantley Adams airport, a multi-lane highway takes visitors to Bridgetown, 15 km away, partly encircling it as it approaches the capital. As opposed to the motorway, the coastal road takes its time to reach the villages as it first winds its way through the cultivated fields that gradually give way to the villages of Maxwell, Dover, St Lawrence, Worthing and finally Hastings, which in recent decades have grown together. A profusion

# MARCO POLO SELECTION: THE SOUTH

**1 Barbados Museum**
Everything about the history, flora, fauna and art of the island (page 38)

**2 Mike's**
Small, hidden restaurant by the ocean (page 45)

**3 Plantation**
Colourful and unforgettable folklore dinner show (page 49)

**4 St Lawrence Gap**
Pure Caribbean nightclub atmosphere is found here (page 49)

**5 Oistins Fish Market**
Fresh fish from the charcoal grill every evening (page 45)

**6 Crane Beach**
Pinkish-white, dream-like beach with palms and waves (page 52)

of smaller hotels and pensions interrupted by a few restaurants and shops line both sides of the highway. One soon gets the impression that the whole southern coast is one single holiday resort, and St Lawrence Gap with its bars, restaurants and nightclubs is its pulsating heart. However, this is not exactly an artificially created holiday enclave, but rather a growing together of Bajan and tourist attractions. The locals also enjoy the amenities of this stretch of coast such as the beach bars and the wonderful beaches, which is exactly what makes the southern coast such an unforgettable holiday experience.

The city centre of Bridgetown begins gradually, almost without transition. The lively business activity seen in the streets of the capital contrasts with the quiet façades of the buildings from whose interiors many important trade decisions are made. On Broad Street, the capital's main shopping artery, countless tourists are seen every day strolling and looking. Their number increases when one or several cruise ships anchor in the harbour and their passengers are then trying to find the ultimate bargain or the most garish T-Shirt. And yet the city has far more to offer.

It comes as a surprise that the city centre has few urban mansions. Instead, colonial buildings and a profusion of colourful wooden houses line the streets, giving the capital a unique atmosphere. The old harbour of Careenage with its many boats is very picturesque, while the lively bustle in and around the bus terminal in Fairchild Market is typically Caribbean. The splendid villas are

seen in the outskirts, often converted to bank or corporate headquarters or even diplomatic representations. One of the best is the one where the Governor-General has his office. The villas soon give way to more modest houses with small gardens until these gradually get lost in the open cultivated fields.

As one moves inland, the landscape is monotonously flat at first. This is where the large plantations are, where sugar cane, cotton and vegetables are cultivated. Several kilometres farther inland, the land finally starts climbing, becoming hilly and more varied.

## BRIDGETOWN

☞ **City Map inside back cover**

(**106/107**) To describe the capital of Barbados as a metropolis or even a big city would be wrong. Instead, it should be called an industrious little city that during busy workdays – especially the early morning hours – seems to groan loudly under the weight of the heavy morning traffic and the unending stream of visitors. The city centre is easily crossed on foot in half an hour. Banks, offices, all kinds of shops, varied markets and bus stations are all close together. The residential areas usually belong to the adjacent parishes, so Bridgetown officially has only approximately 6,000 souls.

Nowhere else on the island is the visitor reminded more of British colonial times than in (**U/D4**) *Trafalgar Square*. This square located in the heart of Bridgetown is as famous as its namesake in faraway London; on top of the high column one can just make out

Admiral Nelson in bronze. There is one important difference, however, one that all Bajans will gladly point out, namely that the colony honoured Nelson's decisive role in the 1805 Battle of Trafalgar a lot earlier than the mother country, erecting the statue in 1813, which was 27 years earlier than in London.

The fountain in front of Nelson's statue has absolutely nothing to do with politics and a lot to do with technical progress. It was commissioned in 1865 to celebrate the introduction of piped drinking water. Another important building on Trafalgar Square is the Parliament Building, a massive structure made of bright coral stone and with wooden blinds erected in 1870.

The first settlers of Barbados landed and settled farther north, in Holetown. Barely one year later, in 1628, they founded Bridgetown. They had found a small wooden bridge that had been used by the original inhabitants of the island to cross the narrowest part of the swampy area of the estuary created by the Constitution River. Thus, they gave this area the name of Indian Bridge Town, later simplified to Bridgetown. Thanks to its protected natural harbour, the city soon began acquiring a certain importance in the region. Nowadays, two bridges cross the inlet.

The inner harbour's former importance is gone, only the name remains. (**U/C-E4**) *Careenage* was the place where the wooden ships once were careened. Back then, the shore was lined with warehouses and docks, still seen here and there. The old cargo sailing ships have been replaced by leisure boats, catamarans and deep-fishing yachts. Still, this colourful and picturesque part of Bridgetown remains quite charming.

Strolling down (**U/C-D4**) *Broad Street,* the capital's main shopping street, one is almost blinded by the profusion of well-decked duty-free shops. The (**U/C4**) *Da Costa Mall* is one that certainly stands out because of its creative way to blend a commercial property with nostalgic elements. Its wedding-cake style façade with its ornate railings and street lanterns inside create an attractive flair which is wholly absent in the sober, unimaginative shopping malls of other places. An additional example of enchanting colonial architecture can be seen in the (**U/C4**) *Barclay Bank* building at the end of the Lower Broad Street. Most of the buildings seen today were built after 1860; the earlier structures were destroyed by hurricanes or fires.

Those who are curious and would like to know what Barbadian housewives buy for their homes should leave Broad Street and walk into one of the parallel streets such as (**U/C3**) *Swan* or *James Street.* At the corner, a Rastafarian offers coconuts; many fruit and vegetable stands line the street. The display windows of the little shops are chock-full of shoes, fabric and everything that the non-tourist needs for everyday life in Barbados.

Apart from the countless duty-free shops, the tourist finds his shopping paradise in the (**106/B3**) *Pelican Village,* a complex of souvenir and handcrafts shops. It is located near the transatlantic harbour, where every morning at

*St Mary's Church, an oasis of tranquillity amid the hustle and bustle of Bridgetown*

least one giant cruise ship is anchored. So that tourists don't get lost on the way to the city centre, a series of T-shirt shops indicate the way.

In this bustling city, the true oases of tranquillity and peacefulness are the varied churches. **(U/E4)** *St Michael's Cathedral* is the most famous of all, especially because it is the largest and second-oldest on the island. It was built between 1784 and 1786 and was one of the very few structures that survived the catastrophic hurricane of 1831. The original **(U/D3)** *synagogue*, at the corner of James Street/Synagogue Lane, had to be completely rebuilt in 1833. Beautifully renovated, it shines magnificently once again. Behind **(U/B3)** *St Mary's Church*, at the end of Lower Broad Street, the 'big city' atmosphere of Bridgetown ends, and small wooden houses characterize the urban scenery. Another historical section can be found east of the city centre, on the southern

coast. A 200-soldier garrison was built here in 1780 in order to protect this prosperous, up-and-coming British colony, especially after the French had lost some of the neighbouring islands and were thinking of re-conquering them. The new garrison was erected in 1705 on one of the ramparts of **(106/C4)** *St Ann's Fort*, the first headquarters. The buildings are a good example of Georgian architecture. The former prison now houses the **(106/C4)** *Barbados Museum.* The most interesting building in the whole complex is undoubtedly the main police station: its red and white colours as well as its yellow-roofed bell tower make it stand out in the distance. No soldiers march on the square opposite the station any more; only cannons stand in rank and file. Normally, it's very quiet here, but on certain days the whole place wakes up: the old parade ground is now the island's racecourse.

Every evening, (**U/B–C1**) *Baxters Road* in the city's north-west section wakes up as well. This is one of the nightlife centres; one *rum shop* after another lines the street. Countless food and beverage street stands look after the hungry and thirsty. The sizzling and boozing typically last well into the night. In the eastern part of the city, nightlife pulsates in the (**U/D–E5–6**) *Bay Street*, the start of the coastal road. The endless bars and clubs by the beach of (**106/C4**) *Carlisle Bay* are particularly attractive.

SIGHTS

**Cockspur Distillery Tour    (106/B2)**
This rum factory has existed for more than 100 years. The 45-minute tour vividly explains the stages in the manufacturing of rum. *Daily 9 am–4 pm, admission 5 Bds$, West Indies Rum Distillery, conspicuously located near the Spring Garden Highway by the beach, Brighton, Black Rock, St Michael*

**Mount Gay Rum Tour    (106/B2)**
The competitor claims to be the oldest rum distillery in the world. It has been making rum from molasses, a byproduct of sugar production, since 1703. The interesting, 30-minute tour gives a very good introduction to the production of the high-proof spirit, although the actual distillery is in the northern part of the island and can't be visited. So the tour, after an introductory film, takes visitors to the warehouse where the rum casks are stored and to the places where rum is blended and bottled. The tour is a rather informal affair and ends with (what else?) a small sample of the product. *Mon–Fri 9 am–4 pm, admission 12 Bds$, Mount Gay Rum Visitors Centre, Spring Garden Highway, Bridgetown*

MUSEUMS

**Barbados Museum    (106/C4)**
★ The former military prison now houses the island's museum. The varied buildings – the ones seen today date back to 1853 and were built in the Caribbean-Georgian style – house many museum pieces pertaining to the geology, flora and fauna, history and art of the little island. However, the display cases containing many

*The charm of yesteryear becomes alive in the Barbados Museum*

stuffed birds, corals, clams, turtles and other creatures, rather than giving valuable insights into the island's natural history, leave visitors rather melancholic. Archaeological finds and articles of everyday use from previous centuries are much more interesting. There are completely furnished rooms, plus historical drawings and paintings which round off the picture of everyday life in colonial Barbados. A room full of silver and crystal ware vividly shows the former wealth of many plantation owners. On the contrary, a prison cell reminds one of the meagre existence of the penitents. There is even a section with old toys. Young visitors can play with some of them and wear a couple of costumes as well. The court garden has a café. For those willing to quench their thirst for knowledge, the library is open from Mon to Fri 9 am–1 pm. *Mon–Fri 7 am–4 pm, admission 12 Bds$, St Ann's Garrison, St Michael*

### Tyrol Cot Heritage Village (106/C2)

This pretty villa was built from blocks of coral and basalt rocks in the northern outskirts of Bridgetown in 1854 and was the residence of Sir Grantley and Lady Adams. After her husband's death, the Lady continued to live in this house until her own death in 1990. From the 1930's to the 1960's, this house was perhaps the most important meeting place of Caribbean politicians. This is where the foundations for the West Indian Federation were laid, whose first and only prime minister was Grantley Adams himself. Most of the furnishings are the original ones; the island's largest sofa, as well as porcelain, antique mahogany furniture, bedrooms, well-stocked bookcases and countless gifts from other countries can be seen inside. The Heritage Village, a complex of souvenir and handcraft shops, consists of some newly built *chattel houses* and is situated within the park. *Mon–Fri 9 am–5 pm, admission 11.50 Bds$, Codrington Hill, St Michael*

## RESTAURANTS

### Bato's Snackette (U/C2)

✹ This inconspicuous restaurant is located right before the Tudor Street becomes the Baxter Road. Most of the patrons are Barbadians who flock here because of the generous helpings of good, plain fare. The day when *coucou* is seen on the lunch menu, all the tables are immediately full. Please note that the 'menu' is no more than just a blackboard hanging from the wall. *Mon–Fri 7 am–4 pm, corner of Reed and Tudor Streets, St Michael, Tel. 426 5834, category 3*

### Brown Sugar (106/C4)

✹ This restaurant is situated not too far from the city centre, on the southern end of Carlisle Bay. Although it offers no view of the ocean, it lies amid a luxuriant tropical winter garden with a pond. It is attractively furnished with rattan. The menu has mostly local dishes; at noon the restaurant offers a planters' buffet with a good selection of typically Bajan and Caribbean dishes, nicely prepared and presented. Some of the dishes are rarely seen specialities. The restaurant is a popular lunch meeting place for Bajans. *Sun–Fri noon–2.30 pm; daily 6 pm–9.30 pm, Aquatic Gap, St Michael, Tel. 426 76 84, category 2*

### Waterfront Café (U/D5)

Directly by the water, this restaurant is a classic of the restaurant trade, so expect large and rather turbulent lunch crowds; the evenings are similar when musicians come to play live. In spite of this, it is still worth visiting – not least because it is the only open-air café in all of Bridgetown that is also located right by the water. You can also sit inside the old warehouse, which is open towards the street. The culinary offerings are extensive, and range from simple sandwiches and salads all the way to elaborate fish and meat dishes. The wrought-iron chairs in front of the unplastered walls decorated with a little bit of art makes this charming place a curious and irresistible mixture of bar and restaurant in spite of all the daily bustle. *Mon–Sat 10 am–10 pm, Bar stays open longer, Careenage, Bridgetown, Tel. 427 00 93, category 2–3*

### SHOPPING

### Cave Shepherd (U/C4)

The island's biggest department store sells things from all corners of the world as well as those articles that make the heart of the tourist beat faster: duty-free perfumes, spirits, sunglasses, cameras, etc., plus souvenirs and a large section having the latest international bathing suit models. *Mon–Fri 8.30 am–5 pm, Sat 8.30 am–1 pm, Broad Str., Bridgetown*

### Colours of De Caribbean (U/D5)

Apart from original leisure fashion clothes with Caribbean patterns and colours, these attractively designed shops also sell some souvenirs. *Mon–Fri 9 am–7 pm, Tues until 10 pm and Thurs until 10.30 pm, Sat 9 am–3 pm, Careenage, beside the Waterfront Café, Bridgetown*

### Julie'n Supermart (U/E4, 107/D2)

In what is presently the largest Caribbean supermarket of all customers can find everything, from mouse traps to all kinds of fiery pepper sauces. *Mon–Sat 8 am–10 pm, Bridge Street, Bridgetown and Hagatt Hall, St Michael*

### Pelican Village (106/B3)

Tourists getting off cruise ships have little time to spare so they like to purchase handcrafts and souvenirs, which is why the approximately 40 pavilions near the harbour have the largest selection in all Barbados. Some of the pavilions don't even bother to open when no cruise ships anchor. *Mon–Sat 9 am–5 pm, Harbour Rd., Bridgetown*

---

**In the spirit of Marco Polo**

Marco Polo was the first true world traveller. He travelled with peaceful intentions forging links between the East and the West. His aim was to discover the world, and explore different cultures and environments without changing or disrupting them. He is an excellent role model for the travellers of today and the future. Wherever we travel we should show respect for other peoples and the natural world.

WWF

### Rasta Market (U/B4)

The Rastafarians sell their wares on street stalls in Cheapside, the name given to the continuation of Broad Street: all kinds of handcrafts are offered for sale, among them leather goods and original souvenirs. Some of them, such as the mahogany carvings, sandals, handbags, armlets, etc. are good alternatives to the mass produced wares offered for sale in the highly commercial Pelican Village. *Mon–Sat 8 am–noon, Cheapside, Bridgetown*

Although Bridgetown is the capital and the business centre of the island, with few exceptions most of the hotels lie somewhat out of town, on the beaches.

### Little Paradise (106/B1-2)

The small, family-run hotel can be found in the northern outskirts of Bridgetown in a quiet neighbourhood. The beautiful *Paradise Beach* can be comfortably reached on foot in only a few minutes; there are also restaurants nearby. Not all of the plainly furnished rooms have balconies and a view of the sea; the hotel itself occupies two buildings separated by a small swimming pool. *18 rooms, Paradise Beach Drive, St Michael, Tel. 424 32 56, Fax 424 86 14, e-mail LittleParadise@caribsurf. com, category 3*

### Savannah (106/C4)

After long and costly renovation, the historical building has been converted into a hotel with all the comforts imaginable; it caters mostly to businessmen. It's located directly opposite the racecourse of Garrison Savannah not far from the Barbados Museum. The city centre of Bridgetown is easily reached and the closest beach is only a short walk away. The hotel has a good restaurant; in the future, a swimming pool as well as another building will be added. *21 rooms, Hastings, Christ Church, Tel. 228 38 00, Fax 228 43 85, e-mail savannah@caribsurf.com, category 2*

Bridgetown is the starting point of all boat tours. Most of them take tourists along the coast to the north. The Hilton Hotel offers many kinds of sports activities; the beach in (**106/C3-4**) *Carlisle Bay* has additional opportunities for the water sports enthusiasts.

### Boat trips

*Atlantis Submarine:* this trip takes place underwater instead of on the water. The submarine has enough room for 28 passengers and dives to reach a coral reef lying at a depth of 50 m. During the journey, the passing fish and the corals are competently described by a diving instructor. This is a great experience, far more dramatic than the routine visit to an aquarium or a ride with a glass-bottom boat. *Shallow Draught, Bridgetown, Tel. 436 89 29.*

❂ *Harbour Master:* the large leisure steamer was originally planned to be a floating casino. The plan came to nothing, so the ship now takes tourists to the west coast during the day; in the evenings, the steamer becomes a floating nightclub. Its traditional dusk trips are popular ways to end the week. Since most of the passengers are Bajans, the trip

*The island's history is retold with music and dancing in the show called '1627'*

will be a good opportunity for observing local colour. *Shallow Draught, Port of Bridgetown, Tel. 430 09 00.*

*Jolly Roger Cruises:* the Jolly Roger is an imitation pirate ship that undertakes 'privateering voyages' to Holetown several times a week. The 'pirates' provide the right atmosphere with the help of Caribbean rhythms and rum punch. Several water sports barely dampen the enthusiasm on board. *Shallow Draught, Port of Bridgetown, Tel. 436 6424.*

Apart from these relatively large ships, there are numerous sailing yachts and catamarans offering sightseeing trips to the west coast: *Limbo Lady Sailing Cruises, Tel. 420 54 18; Small Cats, Tel. 421 64 19 or 231 15 85, Cool Runnings, Tel. 436 09 11, Fax 427 5850; Secret Love Sailing Cruises, Tel. 432 19 72; Tiami Sailing Cruises, Tel. 427 72 45*

### Diving (106/C4)

Introductory diving courses, guided diving excursions and rental of diving equipment: *Dive Shop Ltd., Aquatic Gap, next to Pebbles*

*Restaurant, Tel. 426 9947, e-mail hardive@caribnet.net*

### Beaches

**(106/C3-4)** *Carlisle Bay*, a half-moon-shaped city beach, starts south of the Careenage at the *Boatyacht* beach club and ends at the land tongue occupied by the Hilton. Many sailing yachts anchor here, taking advantage of the protection offered by the bay. Three underwater shipwrecks lure divers and snorkellers. The beach has fine, inviting sand; sun-loungers as well as sunshades can be hired at the Boatyacht. To quench the thirst and pacify the growling stomach, cool drinks and warm dishes can be ordered.

**(106/B1-2)** *Paradise Beach* – this heavenly beach starts immediately north of the harbour. Many locals like to swim there on weekends; during the week, it's mostly empty.

### ENTERTAINMENT

Bajans enjoy going out on Friday and Saturday evenings, but not necessarily to the same disco or nightclub. There is an unwritten rule that visitors looking for the best atmosphere should follow: the crowds will usually flock to the place where live music will be played on that particular night; in addition, it's very important what band will play the music. Therefore, before you leave, it's a good idea to inquire with the Bajans themselves which disco or club is the most popular one for that evening in order to avoid sitting in a deserted establishment totally devoid of atmosphere.

### Boatyacht (106/C4)

◈ ⚓ In the daytime, a beach bar, in the evenings an open-air nightclub and currently one of the hottest addresses in all Barbados. The location on the beach is unique. Live music is played on some evenings; on Tuesdays, when 'all drinks are free', the place bursts at the seams. *Daily from 9 am, admission varies according to evening, Tel. 436 26 22, Bay Street, Bridgetown*

### Harbour Lights (106/C4)

Pub, disco, nightclub – this popular place is all three in one. Live music is offered on several evenings, yet remember that the evenings that are unquestionably 'in' are on Wednesdays and Fridays. The place starts filling up with tourists and locals after 10.30 pm. *Mon until Sat from 9.30 pm, the price of admission varies, Tel. 436 7225, Marine Villa, Bay Street, Bridgetown*

### Harbour Master (106/B3)

You may disagree about its appearance – the rather square-shaped 'Harbour Master' looks more like a floating pontoon than a holiday steamer. While the ship takes tourists up and down the west coast during weekdays, on Friday nights it anchors in front of the harbour and opens up its three decks to the party owls. A restaurant occupies the lowerlevel; above it, there is a dancing area on the open deck. The corresponding weekend programme is announced in the newspaper. *Fri nightclub from 10 pm, Tel. 430 09 00, Shallow Draught, Port of Bridgetown, St Michael*

### 1627 and all that (106/C4)

The attractively mounted folklore show is an excellent dancing and musical introduction to the history of Barbados. The overall quality of the performances is good and avoids the excessive kitsch seen in similar shows trying to imitate Rio's Carnival. Instead, there is more music and even more dancing. A generous buffet featuring many Barbadian specialities and beverages is included in the price of admission. The only drawback: the rather unimaginative and sterile-looking facilities of the conference centre. Free shuttle service to and from the hotel is provided for those who book the show,. *Thurs 6.30 pm, admission 115 Bds$, Barbados Museum, St Ann's Garrison, St Michael, Tel. 428 16 27*

## INFORMATION

### Barbados Tourism Authority

*Mon–Fri 8.30 am–5 pm, Tel. 427 26 23/4, Fax 426 40 80, P. O. Box 242, Harbour Rd., Bridgetown*

# SOUTH-WEST COAST

**(107/D-F5)** The lights of the numerous restaurants by the Bay of St

Lawrence twinkle just as much as the stars high above, as if trying to out-do them. The view from the terrace of a restaurant located directly on the beach encompasses all the way from the pitch-black sea to the myriad colourful lights of the coastal establishments; the waves of the calm tropical sea are heard as they gently splash on the shore. Whether it's fish, steak or pasta, the large culinary selection is tempting indeed. Luckily, European imitations such as schnitzel or *fish and chips* are few and far between. After the sumptuous dinner, the peaceful and warm tropical evening invites one to take a stroll; the boutiques are open late and the countless bars offer relaxation until it's time for the nocturnal revellers to find the closest nightclub and start partying. After all, the atmosphere of the nightclubs doesn't really get going until after 10 pm.

Even if St Lawrence Gap is the island's undisputed entertainment centre, the whole southern coast offers good entertainment as well. For example, the Oistins fish market organizes small-scale public festivals every evening. Just order your delicious portion of fresh fried fish, sit back and listen to the latest calypso and soca rhythms while you take in all the lively bustle around you.

During the day, you can choose from a wide selection of beautiful beaches for sunbathing, swimming and water skiing. If you prefer, you may want to explore all nooks and crannies of this Caribbean jewel from the southern coast: either on your own, or with a hired car or perhaps by bus or even booking one of the many day tours offered. Sometimes it will be hard to make the right choice, especially if your aim is to find the 'true' Caribbean flair without emptying your pocketbook too much.

## RESTAURANTS

This coastal strip offers the biggest selection of restaurants on the island. The offerings range from gourmet cooking with an unforgettable view of the sea to the simple hamburger grill. In between, there are many choices for all budgets.

### Bert's Bar (107/D4)
Garden restaurant and bar for the sports enthusiasts who can watch their favourite tennis matches, car races and other international sports events on the huge satellite TV. Between matches, they can walk over to the numerous slot machines to try their luck. For those who still want to exercise after watching so many sports events, there's a small pool. *Daily 8 am–10 pm, bar until 1 am, Rockley, Worthing, Main Rd.; Christ Church, Tel. 435 79 24, category 3*

### Café Sol (107/D5)
The evening bustle of St Lawrence Gap can be ideally seen from the elevated terrace whilst sipping the latest cocktail creation. The small restaurant with the lemon-yellow façade and interior also offers good, hearty Mexican food such as nachos, burritos, etc. *Daily 6 pm–11 pm, bar stays open longer, St Lawrence Gap, Christ Church, Tel. 435 95 31, category 3*

### Carib Beach Bar (107/D4)
⚘ Popular beach bar directly on the wide, white Sandy Beach next

to the Sandy Beach Hotel. The large bar has some open-air tables on a wooden platform; the palm trees provide some shade. Barbecue on Fridays; on the other days, steaks, fish, shrimp, sandwiches and other tasty dishes. *Daily 10 am–11 pm, lunch from 11.30 am, Fri longer opening hours, 2nd Ave., Worthing, Christ Church, Tel. 435 85 40, category 3*

### Champers                (106/C4)

This restaurant (its subtitle hints at its double nature: *wine bar*) on two levels – the bar downstairs, the restaurant upstairs – is well-lit, nicely furnished and cheerfully decorated. The numerous dishes are very tasty. The menu changes every day and can be read on a large blackboard. The wine selection is especially good, and they can also be drunk by the glass. The sea replaces the usual soft background music, as the restaurant is situated directly by the water. *Mon–Sat noon–4 pm, 6.30 pm until 10 pm, Keswick Building, Hastings, Christ Church, Tel. 435 66 44, category 2*

### Josef's                (107/D4-5)

After costly renovations, Austrian Josef Schwaiger is once again at the helm. Finally, the south coast has an exclusive gourmet address. The atmosphere is stylish and the open-air tables in the large garden by the sea are especially attractive as guests can see and hear the placid waves of the Caribbean as they dine. All dishes are very tasty and nicely prepared, but beware: the portions are typical of the nouvelle cuisine. Advance booking recommended. *Sun–Fri noon–2.30 pm, daily 6.30 pm–10.30 pm, St Lawrence, Gap, Worthing, Christ Church, Tel. 435 65, category 1*

### Mascarade                (107/D4-5)

The impressive menu reads like a trip around the world. The terrace surrounded by all kinds of exotic tropical plants is a welcome quiet refuge from the noisy nightlife of the *St Lawrence Gap, Worthing, Christ Church, daily 6 pm–10.30 pm, Tel. 435 61 04, category 2*

### Mike's                (108/B6)

★ The German Mike Neuhoff runs the place with his Barbadian wife. The small restaurant a little out of the way is located right by the beach. The evening buffets have a different theme every evening. Once you have found the place, you're likely to come back again. *Mon–Sat, buffet from approx. 7 pm, 250 m west of the Silver Sands Hotel by the beach, Christ Church, Tel. 428 86 16, category 3*

### Oistins Fish Market        (107/E-F5)

★ As soon as it gets dark, the little wooden stalls of the Oistins Fish Market change into snack bars. Soon, the smell of grilled fish fillets pervades the air. Customers eat while standing or find some of the few available wooden benches to sit on. This is a typical as well as tasty and reasonably priced culinary experience. *Open from dusk to the early morning hours. The busiest days are Fri and Sat; Main Street, Oistins*

### Red Castle                (107/E-F5)

❖ Directly opposite the Fish Market lies the inappropriately named 'Red Castle' (it's really white) with a bar and a restaurant upstairs. Guests get the feeling they are eating home-cooked food: the good, plain fare is served on washable lace mats. *Daily around the clock, in front of Oistins Fish Market, Tel. 420 63 55, category 3*

### 39 Steps (106/C4)

A striped wooden chest of drawers, green tables and chairs, white tiled floor, many plants – the atmosphere of this bistro is bright and cheerful; the restaurant is a perennial favourite of Bajans as well as foreigners. Guests sit in the airy interior of the upper level of this newly built *chattel house* or outside on the gallery. The daily specials are written on a board; the selection includes quiche and *stuffed crab back* all the way to lasagna – accompanied by a glass of wine with soda water. *Mon–Fri noon–midnight, Sat 6 pm–midnight, Chattel Plaza, Hastings, Christ Church, Tel. 427 07 15, category 3*

### Shak Shak (106/C4)

Its location by the sea is unforgettable. Those who come for lunch are rewarded with reasonable prices and can escape the heat of the midday sun while they fortify themselves with the good food. Reservations recommended for the evening, when the attractive bar invites for relaxation. *Mon–Sat noon–2 pm and 6 pm until 10 pm, Hastings, Christ Church, Tel. 435 12 34, category 1–2*

### Whistling Frog (107/D4-5)

This sports pub offers a really good selection of salads and snacks as well as good, plain Bajan fare. Reasonable prices all day long. *Daily from 7 pm, Time out at the Gap, St Lawrence Gap, Christ Church, Tel. 420 50 21, category 3*

## SHOPPING

### Jam-Pac Music (107/D4-5)

This combined music and souvenir shop specializes in calypso, dub, reggae and gospel. *Mon–Wed 9 am–9 pm, Thurs–Sat 9 am–3 am, beside the After Dark Club, St Lawrence Gap, Christ Church*

### Casuarina Beach Club  (107/D4-5)

The different buildings of these holiday flats are located within a beautifully laid-out tropical garden, where amateur botanists and horticulturists will have a unique chance of admiring some rare species. The studio apartments are well-lit, cheerful and functional; guests can use the kitchen fittings along one wall of the apartment. This hotel is especially popular with families because it offers child care as well as countless sports activities. There is also a large sunbathing lawn and the club's own beach. *160 rooms, St Lawrence Gap, Christ Church, Tel. 428 36 00, Fax 428 19 70, www.barbados.org, category 2*

### Coral House  (108/B6)

The lively German Mike Neuhoff runs this small apartment-hotel located in the southern tip of the island near the Silver Sand Hotel. The spacious 60-square-metre holiday flats have a dining room and a bedroom and are ideal for those who seek a quiet place. Windsurfers also like the location. *10 apartments, Mike Neuhoff, 35 Ealing Park, Christ Church, Tel. 428 86 16 and 428 76 20, Fax 420 80 29, category 3*

### Piech & Quiet  (108/B5)

The attractively furnished, small hotel can be found in the quiet southern tip directly by the sea. It was renovated in the Spanish style and has a restaurant. A swimming pool and the pretty beaches of the vicinity (only a few minutes away) provide relief from the hot tropical climate. *21 rooms, Inch Marlow, Christ Church, Tel. 428 56 82, Fax 428 24 67, www.barbados.org, category 2–3*

### Rostrevor  (107/D-E5)

This hotel located in the very heart of St Lawrence Gap offers a nice family atmosphere in its 1-, 2- or 3-bedroom flats located directly by the beach. With swimming pool. *67 rooms, St Lawrence Gap, Christ Church, Tel. 428 59 20, Fax 428 77 05, www.barbados.org, category 2–3*

### Sand Acres & Bougainvillea  (107/E5)

The hotel lies directly on Maxwell Beach and is famous throughout the island because of its pretty architecture. Its studio holiday flats are very comfortable. *133 rooms, Maxwell Coast Rd., Christ Church, Tel. 428 71 41, Fax 428 25 24, category 1–2*

### Sea Breeze  (107/E5)

The spacious complex has undergone a recent renovation; its pink buildings are located directly on the beach. The restaurant lies exactly between the two main buildings. The *Mermaid* is also famous beyond the confines of the hotel complex. The studio flats have kitchen fittings on one side of the wall. Quite, yet not too far away, located somewhat to the east of St Lawrence Gap. *79 rooms, Maxwell Coast Rd., Christ Church, Tel. 428 28 25/26, Fax 428 28 72, www.barbados.org, category 2*

### Shells  (107/D4)

Rather modest, yet very reasonably priced rooms. A nice restaurant is part of the hotel. The pretty and wide sandy beach is only a stone's throw away. *15 rooms, 1st Ave., Worthing, Christ*

*Alone on the coast: the coast near Oistins*

*Church, Tel. 435 72 53, Fax 435 74 14, category 3*

### Southern Palms (107/D-E5)
This hotel complex is situated in the middle of St Lawrence Gap and consists of seven different buildings. They are cheerfully painted in pink and white and built in the historical colonial style. The guests can enjoy the sports facilities free of charge: tennis courts, mini-golf, snorkelling equipment and windsurfing and boogie boards are offered. *93 rooms, St Lawrence Gap, Christ Church, Tel. 428 71 71, Fax 428 71 75, www.barbados.org, category 1–2*

## SPORTS & LEISURE

The southern coast is the preferred destination for windsurfers. Especially in the winter months, from December to early March, a constant and strong wind blows. But beware: the strong waves and currents are a joy and challenge for the experienced and a frustrating experience for all the others!

### Golf (107/D4)
*Rockley, 9 holes, par 36, Rockley, Christ Church, Tel. 435 78 73*

### Beaches
The south has a wealth of powdery-white beaches consisting of coral sand. Its beautiful beaches are interrupted here and there by a few bays and coves, which give protection from the normally powerful waves coming ashore; the waters are seldom quiet. The prettiest beaches from west to east are: *Rockley,* a lively place full of hawkers and picnic tables; the wide, breakwater-protected *Sandy Beach;* ❖ *Miami* at Oistins, very popular with the locals, and the isolated *Silver Rock Beach* on the southern tip, a windsurfers' paradise.

## Diving

**(107/E5)** *Guide by side* is no large–scale, impersonal diving school. The Austrian Sandrina and her husband Ravi prefer to take care of their clients on an individual basis. *Dover Gardens, Christ Church, Tel./Fax 420 21 35, e-mail sanravi@sunbeach.net.*

**(107/D4-5)** *Exploresub*, well-run PADI-diving establishment located directly on the small bay where St Lawrence Gap begins. *St Lawrence Gap, Christ Church, Tel. 435 65 42, Fax 428 46 74*

## Windsurfing

**(107/E5)** *Club Mistral, Maxwell, Christ Church, Tel. 428 72 77;*
**(108/B6)** *Silver Rock Windsurfing, Silver Sands Beach, Christ Church, Tel. 428 28 66; Silver Sands Resort, Silver Sands, Christ Church, Tel. 428 60 01*

## ENTERTAINMENT

**(107/D5)** ★ *St Lawrence Gap* is the entertainment trip in Barbados. Nowhere else is there so much going on in the evening: restaurants, bars, nightclubs, discos, the selection is huge. A lot of the action takes place out in the open. Bear in mind that in Barbados, a nightclub is not a place where half-naked girls dance. They resemble pubs, and it is recommended that you stop in them only after 10 pm. They fill up only around midnight; many offer live music. As was mentioned before, yesterday's in tips can be outdated today. Before you walk into a nightclub, ask young Bajans when and where there's a lot going on. There's a precise weekly plan for stopping in the different nightclubs.

## After Dark                    **(107/D-E5)**

❂ This large nightclub boasts two fully air-conditioned dance floors, several bars, and an open-air area with a stage on which every Thursday a popular band plays live music. On Fridays and Saturdays, two DJ's provide additional entertainment. The atmosphere of this perennially popular nightclub is sophisticated and relaxed. *Daily from 9 pm, Gateways, St Lawrence Gap, Christ Church, Tel. 435 65 47*

## Plantation                    **(107/D-E5)**

★ While you enjoy the delicious dishes from the generous buffet, you can hear the sounds of a

---

### Signal stations

In the most prominent parts of the island, there are six watch towers that were built in the years of 1818 and 1819. It was decided to build them after the 1816 slave rebellion to improve communications on the island. During the day, flag signals were used; at night, fires. Once the telephone was invented, the towers lost the importance they once had and slowly crumbled away. Some of them, like Gun Hill in St George, Cotton Tower in St Joseph and Grenade Hall were lovingly restored in recent years and are now used as museums or observation towers.

playing steel band. Afterwards, the show begins: a combination of history told in dances and a costume spectacle. The high point of the show is a dancing trip to the celebrations of the Caribbean neighbours, such as the Trinidad carnival. Fire-eaters and limbo round off the programme. The audience sits in a roofed garden restaurant on three levels. Free shuttle service to and from the hotel is provided. *Wed and Fri 6.30 pm with dinner, 7.30 pm with show only, admission with dinner buffet 123 Bds$, show only incl. drinks 60 Bds$, Tel. 428 50 48, St Lawrence Rd., Christ Church*

### Reggae Lounge (107/D-E5)

❂ ☥ As the name already says: Reggae is what matters. Often, live concerts take place here, so inquire. Calypso tunes are also played once in a while. The arena-like building makes it easy for the audience to see and be seen. *Daily from 9 pm, different admission prices. Tel. 435 64 62, St Lawrence Gap, Christ Church*

### Ship Inn (107/D-E5)

This ship is a curious mixture of garden restaurant, bar, nightclub and restaurant. The gastronomic furnishings group around a centrally located inner courtyard – either under open skies or in a closed-in pub. The atmosphere is cosy, the guests come from all places. The Ship becomes an insider's meeting place on Thursdays. *Daily 6 pm–2 am, bar opens at noon, price of admission varies, Tel. 435 69 61, St Lawrence Gap, Christ Church*

## SOUTH-EASTERN COAST

**(108/109)** The region east of the airport is relatively unpopulated compared to the western part. In the district of St Philip, all around the East Cape, only 20,500 people live year-round. The highway ends at the airport, and the small country roads that continue don't follow the coast any longer. The landscape remains flat; during the dry season, only a few shrubs and scorched grass grow. In spite of

*Glistening glamour in the Plantation Dinnershow*

this, the urban expansion slowly continues.

Since the road does not follow the coastline, the beaches can't be seen. It is often necessary to grab a map to try to find out how far you are from the coast. You can also ask the locals or try to follow any road that seems to lead to the coast. However, it's easy to find the *Crane Beach Hotel*, a must-see. White, powdery sand, a dense palm grove and the calm, inviting turquoise waters are ample rewards. This is quite simply one of the most beautiful beaches in all of Barbados. In the south-eastern tip lies the *Sam Lord's Castle*, the island's second-largest hotel, on another one of the island's loveliest beaches. The enormous complex is almost as large as a small city. In front of the walls, outside of the complex, there are a couple of small restaurants. Apart from this, there is nothing else here, and it is still a long way to St Lawrence Gap or the west coast.

## SIGHTS

### Sunbury Plantation House (109/C2)

This impressive plantation house is more than 300 years old and was the island's most visited tourist attraction after Harrison's Cove until 1995, when it burned down completely. In only one year, the house was completely rebuilt and care was taken to furnish it once again with the original antique furniture. Although the lovely charm of yesteryear is gone forever, visitors can now better appreciate how comfortably plantation owners could live in a 'new' plantation house. Apart from the at-

tractively furnished living quarters, the cellar has an interesting display of articles of everyday use. A collection of historical carriages supplements the already interesting tour. Behind the house, a beautiful shady park with a large pond full of water-lilies and a mahogany grove is ideal for strolling. The garden restaurant offers lunch and refreshments. *Daily 9 am–4.30 pm, admission 12 Bds$, St Philip, Tel. 423 62 70*

## RESTAURANTS

### Castle Dinner (109/F2)

His excellency, the pirate Sam Lord, would have been delighted to see that as in previous centuries, guests come to dine in the elegant Regency Room of his castle-like villa. The unscrupulous plantation owner found an additional source of wealth when he got the idea of setting up lights along his stretch of coast to misguide the passing ships so they would run aground. Then, he calmly robbed them. Once a week, guests can partake in the castle's atmosphere while they enjoy the seven-course, 100-US-dollar-dinner. The wine is included in the price. Book the exclusive dinner no later than noon of the same day! *Wed 7 pm, Sam Lord's Castle, St Philip, Tel. 423 73 50*

### Pot & Barrel (109/F2)

❀ In front of the gates of Sam Lord's Castle, there is a cosy and very typical restaurant that instead of serving a pricey seven-course dinner, can offer its guests very tasty Bajan fare for a fraction of the cost: *macaroni-* and *cheese-pie, fried chicken* and fresh fish. *Daily 8 am–10 pm, in front of the entrance to Sam Lord's Hotel, Long Bay, St Philip, Tel. 423 41 07, category 3*

## SHOPPING

### Velda Tyson (109/F2)

Velda makes hand-made articles such as necklaces, earrings and other accessories. She prefers to use only natural materials such as dried fruit, nuts or seeds. *Daily 9 am to 4 pm, in Sam Lord's, her husband manages a selling stand at the Crane Beach Hotel during the midday hours*

## HOTELS

### Crane Beach Hotel (109/E3)

The hotel with the island's best view has a long tradition. It was originally built as a private holiday retreat, later converted to a hotel as early as the late 19th century. Its exposed location on the cliffs give its guests an unparalleled view of the ocean and the wild, picturesque Crane Beach. In previous decades, the world's rich and famous flocked to this exclusive address; nowadays, this magnificent hotel has lost some of its previous lustre. Although the rooms and balconies of the two-storeyed main building are very spacious and comfortable, the furnishings are a bit old fashioned. You will probably recognize the swimming pool, it is often featured in advertisements. An adjacent building with a restaurant and bar was added in the 1960's. The view from it is absolutely wonderful, not even the hotel can compete. It is situated far from the hustle and bustle; for this reason, however, guests have lit-

tle choice other than dining in the hotel restaurant unless they are willing to drive a long stretch. The island's best coconut bread is served for breakfast. *Restaurant daily 8 am–10 am, noon–3 pm, Sun lunch buffet, Mon, Wed, Thurs, Sat, Sun 7 pm–8.30 pm, Fri, Tues until 10 pm with live music, category 1. Hotel 18 rooms, Crane Beach, St Philip, Tel. 423 62 20, Fax 423 53 43, www. barbados.org, category 1–2*

### Sam Lord's Castle (109/F2)

The island's second-largest hotel is located wholly in the southeastern part of the island. It is ideal for those who would like to enjoy all the comforts and luxuries of a first-class hotel amid the tranquillity of its surroundings and the beauty of the beach. The hotel is popular for conferences. Seven tennis courts, five restaurants plus numerous entertainment and sports facilities are offered. The jewel of the entire complex is Sam Lord's Castle, built in 1820 in the Colonial style. It houses the exclusive Regency Room, nine guest's rooms and the reception. *234 rooms, Long Bay, St Philip, Tel. 423 73 50, Fax 423 59 18, www.barbados.org, category 1*

## SPORTS & LEISURE

### Golf (109/E2)

*Belair, 9 holes, par 3, St Philip, Tel. 423 46 53*

### Beaches

The beaches in this part of the island are among the best in all Barbados. From south to north these are: (**109/E3**) *Foul Bay*, an isolated long beach; the two-part ★ (**109/E3**) *Crane Beach*, the island's most beautiful. The white sand is mixed with a little pink and the rather powerful waves come ashore in long and perfectly parallel lines to the slowly sloping shoreline. Some days are ideal for wave riding. Those who want to cross the Crane Beach Hotel to reach the beach must pay 5 Bds$. There is another (free) route to the beach on the other side. (**109/F2**) *Long Bay* is the beach in front of the Sam Lord's. Its relatively protected and the waves are smaller; numerous palm trees line the beach. *Daily 8 am–5 pm, admission 10 Bds$*. Several steps lead to (**109/F1**) *Bottom Bay*. The beach is

approx. 200 m long; a small palm grove clings onto the cliffs behind its back.

### Surfing (109/E3)
Bogieboards can be hired in *Crane Beach*.

**INFORMATION**

### Barbados Tourism Authority
The pavilion in the arrival lounge of the (**108/C4**) Grantley Adams International Airport closes after the last international flight has arrived. *Daily from 8.15 am, Tel. 428 55 70, Christ Church*

*Once a pirate's nest – now an exclusive hotel: Sam Lord's Castle*

# Chic, with luxuriant tropical vegetation

*A perfectly smooth ocean, palms, plus cocktails and candlelight dinners on the beach – the west knows how to spoil its guests*

Although Highway 1 is not exactly a motorway (just a country road), it is nevertheless one of the island's most beautiful roads, as it seems to cross a giant, lush flowering garden. Often, giant-sized gardens resembling parks border the road, their driveways hinting at the luxurious half-hidden villas surrounded by palms and flowering trees. Exclusive names like *Crystal Cove* and *Royal Pavilion* are carved in elegant letters on the entrance walls.

It is here more than anywhere else in Barbados where the most exclusive properties are found, like costly pearls on a string. Here and there, the properties of the well-to-do give way to more modest housings, the neat and original *chattel houses*; often, their occupants put all their love into them and into their small but neat front gardens as if competing to be the island's most beautiful.

*The entire west coast is a long, single beach: postcard idyll on the Alleynes Bay*

At times, one gets a short but lovely glimpse of the coast; the placid, blue Caribbean Sea seems to be asleep under the hot tropical sun. Palms and other trees grow within a few feet of the water, providing welcome shade from the midday heat. Not far away skillful Barbadian hands quickly cut up the dark red meat of a silvery fish – idyllic impressions from the most picturesque coastal highway in Barbados, providing the visitor with one enchanting tropical view after another.

The western coast of Barbados comprises the administrative district of St James (approx. 21,000 inhabitants), the smallest yet prettiest in the whole island. Although most of the luxurious villas on the beach are owned by wealthy foreigners, many Bajans still live in their neat *chattel houses*, sometimes even beside the giant properties, hopefully they won't be pushed out of them in the near future. It is exactly this odd mixture of Hollywood-like villas and exclusive hotels standing next to small, colourful wooden houses, all surrounded by the lovely-lush tropical vegetation which makes the west coast so irresistibly attractive.

Those who spend their holidays here do so on a grand scale. Almost all of the hotels situated here offer a high standard and magnificent opportunities for all kinds of water sports. The beaches are immaculate, though not very wide. In a nutshell: those who prefer a placid sea rather than the excitement of heavy surf are in the right spot.

Perhaps the best way to get to know this stretch of coast is by walking along the beach, what the locals call *hotel watching*. Since all beaches in Barbados must remain open to the public, one can get a good glimpse of the island's most exclusive properties and swim in their beaches even if one's own accommodations are decidedly more modest.

For the most part, holiday activities are restricted to the hotels and restaurants, many of which are beautifully located on the beach. In fact, apart from Holetown, there is no other village where one could stroll in the evening. In spite of this, and even if you have only booked half-board,

by all means try out some of these restaurants. After all, do keep in mind that the very best ones are located on the western coast; take advantage of the fact that some hotels don't force their guests to take their meals there – half-board notwithstanding – but give them the option to eat out once in a while.

An evening with live entertainment featuring music and shows is the standard programme in the large hotels. Adventurous ones who would like to see real Barbadian nightlife should go to Bridgetown or to the southern coast instead. The only exception is the Coachhouse.

In the centre of the west coast lies *Holetown*. This is the place where the first British settlers landed in 1627. Nowadays, Holetown is the most popular destination of virtually all boat tours, and especially of the 'Jolly Rogers' pirate ship. It anchors here every day at lunchtime so its passengers can sample the various specialities offered in the historical town. Apart from this, few things remind visitors of the historical event. Nevertheless, every February, a large festival honouring the first settlers takes place here.

Originally, the settlers named it St James Town, in honour of the British monarch; later the name was changed to Holetown to remind everyone of 'The Hole' on the Thames. Just like in the mother country, ships having a low draught could sail into the river – today it looks more like a stream. The old part of the village boasts just a couple of old houses and a pretty church. The main reason most visitors come to Holetown, though, is not because they want to learn about the island's history, but because this place is the undisputed culinary centre of this stretch of coast.

Just a few miles northwards lies another important attraction, the *Royal Westmoreland Golf Course*. Even those who are not golfers should visit the impressive complex – or at least see it from the side road that borders the greens.

Yet the west isn't just a golf course or a stretch of coast; the interesting and varied hinterland of St Thomas (pop. about 11,600) offers several caves with interesting formations, gorges filled with dense tropical vegetation, endless sugar cane plantations as well as unsurpassed views from the island's two highest peaks, the Mount Misery (328 m) and the Mount Hillaby (340 m). Whereas Mount Misery is easily recognized by its profusion of antennae on its summit, the search for Mount Hillaby is a more interesting one. Where are the signs leading to it? Those are easily overlooked. At least you could ask how to get there, and in the process learn about village life on the island. Surrounding the mountains (or rather hills) are a good many settlements full of picturesque *chattel houses*; the search for the prettiest one will make you forget the everyday stress of the typical First World metropolis.

*The dining-room of the plantation owner – Francia Plantation*

When you have finally arrived at your destination, you will see Barbados down below – at least its eastern half. Chances are, you'll be the only one here, as the more popular observation point is farther southward, namely *Gun Hill Tower and Signal Station*.

## SIGHTS

### Francia Plantation          (103/E6)
The most interesting sight of this large plantation still in use (it's here where most of the island's *hot pepper* is cultivated) is the plantation home. It is still owned by the descendants of the founder. Although there are other, much older plantation homes on Barbados, this is one of the very few that is always open to the public. It was built in the early 20th century and shows a blend of French and Bajan architectural styles. The wide outside staircase leads visitors to an en-trance hall whose floor and walls are made of the dark Brazilian hardwood *sucupira*. In the middle there is a Victorian 'loveseat' for the chaperone. The adjacent living and dining room is still furnished with the original pieces – some of the most beautiful furniture dates back to the 19th century and was made from local mahogany. In addition, an interesting collection of old maps and watercolours showing Bajanian motifs can be seen. From the back veranda one can get a very good view of the large, terrace like garden. *Mon–Fri 10 am–4 pm, admission Bds$ 9, Tel. 429 04 74 near Gun Hill Signal Station, St George*

### Gun Hill          (103/E6)
Almost nothing changes as the centuries go by: the view from the signal and watchtower of St George, the most important of six *signal stations*, is still magnificent. In previous centuries, flags of dif-

*Harrison's Cave provides a unique glimpse of underground Barbados*

ferent colours were used as signals to warn ships of impending dangers. The view from above is so good that you can see the coastal plain all the way to Bridgetown. Many of the cruise ship passengers can even recognize their ship anchored in the harbour! The tower was built by the British in 1818 and was restored in 1982. Apart from the view, there is an old cannon on top and a collection of military keepsakes. *Mon–Sat 9 am–5 pm, admission 10 Bds$, St George*

## Harrison's Cave          (103/D–E4)

The large, impressive cave with many formations lies exactly in the geographical centre of the island, and close to the highest point as well. The tour of the cave is done with a little railway; the 1.5-km-long journey is accompanied by the sound of the splashing water coming from numerous underground streams, which now and then build small ponds or even flow from one level to another as miniature waterfalls. At the lowest point, the water comes down a full 14 metres! The most impressive room is the so-called 'Cathedral'. The real stars of the show are the beautiful stalagmites and stalagtites, and as such they are effectively lit by powerful lights. *Daily 9 am–4 pm, admission 15 Bds$, St Thomas, on Highway 2*

## Welchman Hall Gully          (103/D4)

★ Not far from Harrison's Cave, situated among the hills of St Thomas, there is a second natural wonder. At an altitude of 270 m, there is a large fracture in the earth, 15 m deep and 1.25 km long, which the locals call *gully*. The *gullies* are created by the forces of nature when the roof of

an underground stream collapses. Some of them have a depth of 60 m! Owing to the island's characteristic limestone layer, there is an extensive underground river system as rainwater easily filters through the porous limestone. Perhaps the best place to see this phenomenon is in Harrison's Cave. In the past, these *gullies* served as natural borders delimiting the plantations. Perhaps the most interesting of all is Welchman Hall Gully, a real treasure trove of rare plants and geologic formations. This is the way Barbados looked when the first white settlers arrived. The leisurely half-hour walk takes visitors along a 1.25-km-long, winding path that passes by impressive bamboo groves, high palm trees, the 'bearded' fig trees, impenetrable bushes and exotic tropical flowers. If you are lucky you may see groups of monkeys swinging from tree to tree. The gorge has two entrances and extends a little beyond Harrison's Cave. Trees and plants have signs with numbers on them, so they can be easily identified with the help of a small brochure handed out at the entrance. Sometimes, though, the person in charge forgets to do so. Be sure you ask for it! ✧ An additional attraction of this tour is the magnificent view of the eastern coast from the northern entrance. *Daily 9 am–5 pm, admission 12 Bds$, on highway 2 near Harrison's Cave, St Thomas*

### MUSEUM

## Sir Frank Hutson Sugar Museum & Seasonal Factory Tour   (102/B–C4)

★ The *Portvale Sugar Factory* is the largest of the sugar factories still in use. During the short season, from February to May, visitors can see how the plant is processed to yield sugar and other important derivatives such as molasses – an important ingredient for the manufacturing of rum. The small museum vividly displays the impact that this giant grass had on the history and society of the island. Drawings, old machines and tools make history and the sugar refining process come alive. The museum is open all year. The visit is even more interesting during the sugar harvest, when the factory is also open to guided tours. The well-informed guides explain all the processing steps needed to produce the tiny sugar crystals. *Mon–Sat 9 am–5 pm, admission 15 Bds$ incl. tour of the factory, 5 Bds$ only for the museum, beside Highway 2a, St James*

## RESTAURANTS

The island's very best restaurants are situated on the west coast. The selection is wide; many restaurateurs know how to maintain their reputation. In spite of this, things can change, as one top chef can leave the kitchen of a top-rated restaurant and go to the competition or even become independent and open his own establishment. Therefore, you'll do well to study as well as try out the selection.

Most of the restaurants lie directly on the beach, so they naturally have magnificent views. In addition, all top-rated hotels have their own outstanding restaurants; some of them even offer their guests having booked half-board the opportunity to sample the food of other neighbouring restaurants chosen by the hotel at no extra charge. It's a great and very popular idea, which gives tourists the opportunity to widen their culinary experience.

A true Bermuda Triangle is Holetown. In an area delimited by two longitudinal streets and two additional ones at right angles to them, there are a total of about ten restaurants! There is a restaurant for every pocketbook but expect to pay more for the higher quality offered here.

### Bombas                            (102/A-B5)

Not a world-class restaurant, but a rustic beach bar in a wonderful location. Popular meeting place during the happy hour. All dishes under 20 Bds$: pasta, curry dishes, vegetarian dishes, chicken, fish, hamburgers and snacks. *Tues–Sun 11 am–midnight, Paynes Bay (north of the Beachcomber Apartments), St James, Tel. 432 05 69, category 3*

### Cliff                              (102/A-B5)

A unique theatrical atmosphere: the semi-circular stalls lie higher than the parquet, and the sea is the torch-lit stage. Every evening, the same well-rehearsed performance takes place: the indescribably delicious and very unusual dishes come to your plate in creative presentations. To top it off, service is friendly and efficient. You will have a hard time deciding between duck breast or jumbo shrimp in vermouth sauce. Book several days in advance. *Mon–Sat 6.30 pm–10 pm, closed in June, Derricks, St James, Tel. 432 19 22, category 1*

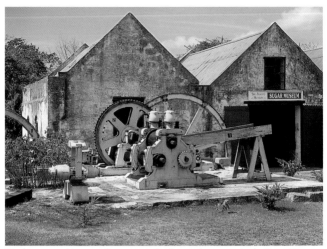

*You learn everything you always wanted to know about sugar in the Sugar Museum*

## Fathoms (102/A-B5)

★ You hear the roaring of the waves, see a magnificent fig tree by the beach, sit comfortably on padded chairs. The atmosphere is perfect, the food couldn't be better. For a start, warm bread and butter, to be followed by *blackened shrimps* with mangoes, *ginger prawns à la Bali* or *cashew speckled kingfish* in mustard sauce – the dishes prepared here are creative as well as delicious. Something else should be praised, too: wine is also served in half-bottles. Advance booking recommended. Upstairs is the *Revolution Café* serving drinks. *Daily noon–3 pm, 6.30 pm–9.30 pm, the bar opens around 11 am, Paynes Bay, St James, Tel. 432 25 68, category 2*

## Indigo (102/A4)

Jason and Nick, two young and creative restaurateurs decided to open their own establishment after working in some of the best first-class restaurants for years. Their restaurant decorated in bistro-style impresses because of its airy look. The light food reflects international influence. Many fish dishes. The popular bar becomes very crowded on weekends, so advance booking is recommended. *Mon–Thurs 6 pm–1 am, Fri/Sat from 6 pm, open closing time, Holetown, St James, Tel. 432 29 96, category 2*

## Mews (102/A4)

A well established restaurant serving outstanding food made with fresh fish and fresh ingredients. The specialities are sashimi prepared with fresh local fish and *lemon shark* – the menu is updated daily. Guests sit in a roofed inner courtyard with rough-plastered walls surrounded by lush decorative plants or upstairs in small rooms with open windows. The comfortable bar by the entrance has become a very popular meeting place in the late evening hours. Good wine selection; advance booking recommended. *Mon–Fri noon–3 pm, Mon–Sat 7 pm–10.30 pm, 2nd Street, Holetown, St James, Tel. 432 11 22, category 1–2*

## Olives (102/A-B4)

This restaurant in Holetown occupies an imposing, historical house on a corner; the structure is made of solid coral stone and has green lattice windows and a narrow, circular balcony. The programme: a bar and a bistro under the same roof, although it should be added that the 'bistro' is a vast understatement. Guests dine either in the garden or in the pretty, high-ceilinged guest room. The kitchen prepares Caribbean-Mediterranean dishes; examples are the hot Jamaican *jerk pork*, pizza and tuna fish *carpaccio*. In the cosy and airy bar upstairs featuring a sitting area, oriental rugs and an indoor palm tree, the hours go by quickly; the short rendezvous easily becomes a long evening in part owing to the talented barman who really knows how to mix and pour. *Daily 6.30 pm until 10.30 pm, the bar stays open longer, 2nd Street, Holetown, St James, Tel. 432 21 12, category 1–2*

## Raffles (102/A-B4)

The memory photo taken in front of the big zebra inside Raffles is part of the unforgettable evening as is the sherbet served between the courses. The theme is Africa, and all the furnishings and decoration remind one of the Dark Continent: a lot of white varnished wood, sitting cushions with leopard patterns, 'wild' animals used for decoration – granted, the furnishings are kitschy but somehow attractive. Many of the dishes

served here are prepared *à la nouvelle cuisine bajanne*: deliciously full-flavoured and refined. The dining room is air-conditioned. Advanced booking recommended. *Tues–Sun 7 pm–10 pm, 1st Street, Holetown, St James, Tel. 432 65 57, category 1*

## Ragamuffins (102/A-B4)

Inside this *chattel house* with green interiors and a small veranda eight tables barely fit in. Their closeness as well as the table cloths with flower patterns make this unusually cosy and attractive. A large fishing net hangs from the ceiling. From the dining room, the eyes can wander to the barstools and get a glimpse of the kitchen. The musical background is provided by Bob Marley's 'Rastaman'. The menu is fully Caribbean. Try the *blackened* fresh fish served with fried *plantains. Mon–Sat 6.30 pm–9.30 pm, bar from 5 pm, 1st Street, Holetown, St James, Tel. 432 12 95, category 2*

## The Restaurant (102/B4)

Even if the Sandy Lane Hotel is presently being renovated, the epicurean spirit of its very famous restaurant lives on in the golf club. The menu is always changing; on Sundays there is a buffet accompanied by jazz and steel band music.*Tues–Sun 7 am–9.30 pm, Sandy Lane Golf-Club, Sandy Lane, St James, Tel. 432 28 38, category 1*

SHOPPING

## Chattle House Village (102/A-B4)

The village consists of several cottages offering all kinds of souvenirs for sale. There is also a delicatessen with tasties from all corners of the world. *Varied opening times, Holetown, St James*

### Earthworks Pottery (102/C5)

Pottery with many different patterns and in all shapes and sizes for all tastes and pocketbooks is offered for sale here. Blue and its many hues is the favoured colour. The workshop and adjacent shop are a little out of the way in the interior, but the trip is well worth it. *Mon–Fri 9 am– 5 pm, Sat 9 am–1 pm, Edgehike Heights 2, St Thomas*

### Gatsby Boutique (102/A3)

Exquisite ladies' and men's wear featuring the creations of international fashion designers – this is the right address for all those who have pocket money to spare and want to purchase the latest creation during their holiday in the tropics. Several branches in the hotels, but the best selection is in the *Royal Pavilions (see hotels), Mon–Fri 10 am–6 pm, Sat 10 am–2 pm*

### Gaye Boutique (102/A-B4)

Highly original beach and leisure fashion of excellent quality. The fair prices make this an ideal place for rummaging. *Mon to Fri 9 am– 5 pm, Sat 9 am–1 pm, Holetown, St James*

### Simons (102/A5)

British designer Simon Foster settled down in Barbados a long time ago. He likes to work particularly with natural materials. His creations are well-known throughout the island and beyond. *Mon– Fri 9 am–5 pm, Sat 10 am–1 pm, closed in June (opposite the Treasure Beach Hotel), Payne Bay, St James*

## HOTELS

The character of the west coast dictates the kind of holiday resorts and retreats. Here are some of the best hotels in all the Caribbean. In between the luxurious palaces are some smaller and more reasonably priced accommodations, but they are few and far between. If the quoted prices seem exorbitant at first, do keep in mind that some of the top-rated hotels also lower their prices as part of a packaged tour.

### Colonial Club (102/A3)

Spacious hotel occupying a very beautiful, quiet stretch of beach north of Holetown. The enormous palms tower over the two-storeyed structure built in the colonial style. The rooms have their own access to one of the four swimming lagoons, which look more like streams than pools. The garden full of lush tropical vegetation opens out towards the sea. The open-air restaurant with its *Orchid Room* serves good food in a magnificent setting. There are tennis courts and a fitness room. Guests are allowed to use the facilities of all the other St James Hotels. *98 rooms, Porters, St James, Tel. 422 23 35, Fax 422 06 67, category 1*

### Crystal Cove (102/A6)

★ The two-storeyed holiday apartments are found scattered on a slope. Brightly painted in white with turquoise, lilac and pink spots, they blend perfectly with all the tropical plants and high palms. The view from most of the large balconies is outstanding: the calm, aquamarine waters of the Caribbean can be admired whilst relaxing on the balcony hammocks. The rooms are exquisitely and elegantly furnished, with large mirrors and décor made of fabric; their brightness

*The Crystal Cove is the start of the luxurious hotels of the west coast*

and cheerfulness mirror their tropical setting. A waterfall divides the bar from the swimming lagoons resembling tropical streams. The facilities offered on the pretty beach include water skiing, windsurfing, kayaking, sunfish- and catamaran sailing as well as snorkelling. All are free of charge for the guests; diving can be arranged. Restaurant and beach bar. The facilities of the other three St James Hotels can also be used free of charge by the guests. A free water-taxi takes people from one hotel to another. *88 rooms, Appleby, St James, Tel. 432 26 83, Fax 432 82 90, category 1*

### Europa (102/A-B4)

This holiday apartment complex can be found in the middle of the luxurious villas of Sunset Beach. The rows of bungalows make a curve around the swimming pool. The rooms are somewhat plain, but they offer a good alternative to those tourists who want to spend their holidays on the western coast but don't want to pay exorbitant prices. Keep in mind, though, that it can get very hot here, as there is no breeze coming from the sea. A restaurant is within the complex. Shopping nearby. Other similar apartments managed by the same company are in the vicinity. *49 rooms, Homar Rentals Ltd., Europa, Palm Avenue, Sunset Crest, St James, Tel. 432 67 50, Fax 432 72 29, category 2-3*

### Mango Bay (102/A4)

This small, all-inclusive semi-luxurious hotel of the medium-priced range is located in the centre of Holetown, directly on the busy beach. Good sports facilities; all rooms with TV. The suites face the sea and are very pretty. The wine on the tables of the hotel-owned, open restaurant are not included in the price. The walls are oddly decorated with painted mango trees. It is also possible to eat in other places. *64 rooms, 2nd Street, Hosetown, St James, Tel. 32 13 84, Fax 432 52 97, www.barbados.org, category 1 (all-inclusive)*

### Royal Pavilion (102/A3)
North of Holetown, on Alleynes Bay, the luxurious Royal Pavilion and its sister hotel named Glitter Bay enjoy the rather exclusive privilege of having no immediate neighbours. Both hotels are within a large park and were built in the colonial style; the main colour in use is pink. The room complex faces the sea, so that the view from the spacious room patios is unforgettable. Two restaurants lie directly on the beach as well. The *Palm Terrace* is a tastefully decorated gourmet restaurant; tea is served every afternoon in the adjacent lounge. The beach in front of the hotel is rather narrow, but a much wider bay lies next to it. The swimming pool is rectangular, ideal for swimming laps. There are also 2 tennis courts and full water sports facilities for the guests; only diving is extra. *72 rooms and a villa with 3 rooms, Pemberton Hotels, Porters, St James, Tel. 422 55 55, Fax 422 39 40, www.cphotels.com, category 1*

### Sandpiper Inn (102/A4)
The two brightly coloured, two-storeyed structures resemble bungalows with gabled roofs and feature spacious terraces or balconies.

Attractive wood was used throughout. There is a garden between the living units and the beach. A wooden footbridge separates the garden from the beach. Right in the middle is the nice, open restaurant. This attractive hotel is centrally situated, directly on the beach of Holetown. Windsurfing, sailing and snorkelling is available to all hotel guests free of charge. *45 rooms, St James Beach, St James, Tel. 422 22 51, Fax 422 17 76, www.barbados.org, category 1*

### Settlers Beach (102/A4)
The villas spread out within a large garden that meets the beach of Holetown. All one- or two-bedroom apartments are luxuriously furnished. There is also a first-class French restaurant within the hotel complex. In addition, a swimming pool. Special prices for families. *22 cottages, Holetown, St James, Tel. 422 30 53, Fax 422 19 37, www.barbados.org, category 1–2*

### Smuggler's Cove (102/A-B5)
Not very pretty, but functional: this middle-priced hotel towers three storeys above the beach and was built at a right angle to it. The rooms are modestly furnished with rattan; there is also a cooking area. As if to compensate for the plain hotel architecture, the beach in front of it is one of the prettiest on the entire western coast. Pool, restaurant. *21 rooms, Paynes Bay, St James, Tel. 432 17 41, Fax 432 17 49, category 2*

### Tamarind Cove (102/A-B4)
This is the biggest of all the St James Hotels. Those who stay here can enjoy all the facilities of this and all the other hotels free of charge. The buildings resem-

ble Spanish haciendas and lie parallel to the big, 250-m-long hotel beach; 4 pools are in the garden between hotel and beach; there is a fitness centre, too. Several restaurants, among them is the one specializing in seafood, appropriately named *Neptune*. A perfect hotel for families. *166 rooms, Tel. 432 13 32, Fax 432 63 17, category 1*

Water sports are offered by virtually all hotels. In addition, guests can hire jet skis or they can also *ride* on the pillion seat. The best time of the day for this and for water skiing is in the morning, when the placid water is as smooth as glass.

### Golf (102/B2-3)

*Royal Westmoreland Golf & Country Club*: The 27-hole-golf course, par 72, was designed by world-famous architect Robert Trent Jones Jr. and is the island's most beautiful. (*Westmoreland, St James, Tel. 422 46 53*); and *Sandy Lane Hotel & Golf Club*, 18-hole golf course, par 72 (*St James, Tel. 432 1311*)

*Holetown Beach, where the first settlers landed in 1627*

## Horseback riding (103/E5)

*Beau Geste Stables*, for advanced horseback riders. *Allison Cox, The Hope, St George, Tel. 429 01 39*

## Beaches

The entire west coast is one big beach. The stretch of white sand is interrupted only by a few rocks, so anyone can run without obstacles from Colony Club northwards. Since the coastline follows the slightly curved bays and coves, the landscape is never monotonous. Particularly beautiful is *Paynes Bay* at the Treasure Beach Hotel, also *Sandy Lane Bay* at the Sandy Lane Hotel, which is being totally renovated. Also worth seeing is the northern end of Holetown Bay at the Colonial Club. The beach is sometimes narrow and sometimes wide, but it always drops slightly and the water is invitingly calm owing to the offshore reefs. However, in some places, corals can hinder an easy approach to the water.

## Diving (102/A4)

The off-shore coral reefs that act as breakwaters are often very pretty; the wreck of the Greek freighter 'Stavonikita' is a major diving attraction. Many diving schools have established themselves along the coast. The recommended ones close to the 'Stavo' and the reefs are: *West Side Scuba Centre, Baku Beach, Holetown, St James, Tel./Fax 432 25 58*

## ENTERTAINMENT

## Casbah Nightclub (102/A4)

An imaginatively decorated disco, it is the most popular on the west coast. The long, curved counter is ideal for meeting people; the sitting furniture decorated with Oriental motifs is perfect for long and undisturbed chatting. There is live music on some evenings. *Daily 10 pm–4 am, Baku Beach, Holetown, St James, Tel. 432 22 58*

## Coach House (102/B5)

✪ ⚲ This little brother of the *Ship In* of St Lawrence Gap is the only real nightclub in the whole western coast – apart from those inside the hotels, that is. There is music every evening – but it is mostly taped. Therefore, it pays to wait until Thursday, when there is dancing. In spite of these shortcomings, the atmosphere here is more informal and personal than in many other nightclubs on the south coast. There is also a bit of food, of course. For more substantial meals, walk over to the adjacent restaurant *Island*, open *daily from 6.30 pm until 10.30 pm. Tel. 432 28 19, The Verandah & Garden, 6 pm–11 pm.* Free taxi-shuttle service from and to the hotels of the west coast. *Daily 6 pm until 2 am, Sun-Fri lunch noon–2.45 pm, Paynes Bay, St James, Tel. 432 11 63*

## Crocodile's Den (102/A–B5)

✪ The attractive *chattel house* is a popular meeting place for nocturnal revellers and billiard-players. On Fridays and/or Saturdays the 'Fiesta Latina' takes place; non-stop dancing accompanied by the hottest rhythms. *Daily from approx. 5 pm until the last guest leaves, Tel. 432 76 25, opposite the Treasure Beach Hotel, St James*

# A wild and unspoiled landscape

*This interesting part of the island is full of contrasts: heavy surf, empty beaches, strangely shaped hills, the raw force of the Atlantic in the North Cape and the idyllic Caribbean in Speightstown*

After thousands of miles of open waters, the powerful waves of the Atlantic finally reach the shore, crashing with full force into the isolated offshore cliffs. Then the rumbling, roaring surf finally comes to rest on the tropical beach, and as it does, a salty mist fogs up the air, softening the mild evening light even more and making the palm fans glisten smoothly as the soft evening breeze moves them gently back and forth. The hills that not long ago were so close, now look deceivingly far away. This wild, romantic scenery is very real and is found every day in and around Bathsheba, the little village situated in the middle of the east coast. This is the spot where the powerful Atlantic waves, pushed by the trade winds for countless miles, finally meet the land. A couple of eroded cliffs testify to the mighty, endless battle of the elements that for hundreds of thousands of years has been enacted here.

*Tent Bay – not far from Bathsheba*

North of Bathsheba, the white tongues of the surf lick the long, seemingly endless white beach. The offshore coral reefs are seen only for short periods; they are treacherous obstacles rightfully feared by most swimmers. Nevertheless, bold surfers defy the dangers of this wild, romantic coast and ride the powerful, high waves.

The east coast of the island is almost unpopulated. Apart from Bathsheba, the only other settlement that deserves the name of a village is Belleplaine. The two *parishes* of St Joseph (approx. 7,600 inhabitants) and St Andrew (approx. 6,300 inhabitants) are the least populated in Barbados. Whereas Bathsheba has some tourism infrastructure in the form of modest accommodations and restaurants, farther north there are no facilities whatsoever, making this the place to go to experience true, original Barbadian landscape.

The hinterland of Bathsheba is characterized by gentle hills. Their green slopes are covered by high coconut palms and massive banana trees. Farther northwards, the lush tropical vegetation slowly gives way to a landscape of bizarre sandstone formations, which in turn is replaced by low, green hills. You have now arrived at the appropriately named *Scotland District*. Sure enough, the rounded green hilltops remind the visitor of far-away Scotland except for the temperature and the tropical fruit plantations of mango and Barbadian cherry trees growing in the secluded valleys down below.

Farther to the north, the island gets flatter. Here, in St Lucy (pop. approx. 9,500), large sugar cane plantations characterize the surrounding landscape; farther northwards these give way to cattle farms and greenhouses. Finally, the northern end of the island is reached, but no inviting beaches are found anywhere: the coast is wild and rugged and the high salt content of the strong prevailing winds allows only sparse vegetation to grow. At the North Cape or the picnic spot at River Bay you can feel the force of the wind as you breathe the pure, oceanic breeze whilst you admire this primeval landscape.

Listening to the heavy surf and feeling the misty, salty spray on your face you may forget for an instant that you are in a Caribbean island after all.

South of *Harrison Point Lighthouse,* located on the north-western coast, the landscape gradually becomes typically Caribbean. Once again, in the lee side of the wind, the familiar scenery known so well from the south-west coast reappears: palm trees, white beaches, calm turquoise waters. In the middle of this lovely landscape is Speightstown, situated in the St Peter parish, the only one with two coastlines. In spite of this beauty, so far the relatively long distance to Bridgetown and to the international airport have prevented large-scale tourism development in this area. Thus, this stretch of coast boasts more fishing villages than hotels or even restaurants!

The landscape south of Bathsheba on the east coast is charming and varied as well. The land slopes down relatively steeply from an elevation of 300 metres to the coast. Here, ᘐᐧ *Hackleton's Cliff* offers some of the very best views

# MARCO POLO SELECTION: THE NORTH-EAST

**1 Round House**
The 'in-place' in Bathsheba (page 75)

**2 Sea-U**
Small, charming pension with a fantastic view of the sea (page 77)

**3 Bath Recreation Park**
A pretty beach with casuarinas providing shade (page 77)

**4 Cattlewash Bay**
Sand and waves as far as the eye can see (page 77)

**5 Farley Hill National Park**
This former film set remains an enchanting place (page 79)

**6 Mango's by the Sea**
Relaxed dining on the veranda (page 81)

in all of Barbados. It's even possible to see the pitiful remains of the large forest that once covered the entire island. In the hinterlands of St Joseph and St John, large agricultural estates (some with well-preserved plantation homes) once again dominate the scenery of this part of the island.

The coastal road soon moves inland. To the left and right, extensive banana and sugar cane plantations cover the rolling hills. Here and there, a glimpse of the coastline reveals picturesque fishing villages located on enchanting coves such as *Martins* or *Consett Bay*. Between them lies the pretty beach of *Bath*, a favourite weekend destination for all Barbadians in search of relaxation.

It is here in north-eastern Barbados where the true face of the island is best seen; there are many interesting places to visit – plenty of reasons to explore this primeval part of the island, either individually or as part of a day tour. Maybe you will even be in the mood to spend a few days in the placid atmosphere of the northern or eastern coast.

# BATHSHEBA AND THE EAST

(**104/105**) Nestled into the green slopes, many typical *chattel houses* have become a part of the lush tropical landscape. The high palms, banana trees as well as all kinds of brightly coloured tropical flowers seem to swallow up the tiny houses. The road follows the coast only for a short period; soon, the hills force the road to move steeply inland. In a short time, you are in Bathsheba: a small bar, a nondescript supermarket, an old man dozing in front of his house – Bathsheba is a dreamy place. Most of the tourists come to the village from the south in order to see the dramatic scenery of the so-called *soup bowl*, a coastal formation where the roaring sea waves collide with several picturesque monoliths. Needless to say, this is one of the island's favourite photo motifs; few stay overnight, though.

It comes as a surprise to know that in the early part of the century, this village enjoyed great popularity; as a matter of fact it even had a railway station. The reason: in the days before air-conditioning, this was the coolest spot on the island. The only thing that has remained from the 'good old days' is the ruined railroad bridge that once crossed Joe's River. Since then, the different and wild scenery, as well as the pure, salty breeze – and most certainly the lack of any hustle and bustle – have made this spot the preferred destination of stressed Bridgetowners. The high point of the outing with the whole family or group of friends is the relaxed, substantial lunch at the Edgewater Inn or the Atlantis.

North of the actual Bathsheba, on Cattlewash Bay – exactly where the long sandy beach starts –, well-to-do Bajans have built their holiday houses into the loose sand of the beach. They remind you of the Californian beach houses; some of them are even rented to foreigners during the off-season.

## SIGHTS

### Andromeda Botanic Gardens (104/B3)
This beautiful botanical garden occupies an entire slope and is

built on terraces. Winding, attractively laid out footpaths take visitors to the different parts of the garden. In the lower part, a profusion of different palm trees can be admired, while the upper part consists of a colourful bougainvillea grove providing a full range of reddish and pink hues. In between, there are enchanting meadows and tranquil ponds as well as arboreal giants providing welcome shade from the hot tropical sun. In addition, there are many different kinds of cacti and hibiscus, succulents and ferns – the founder of this botanical marvel was Iris Bannochie, who brought thousands of plants from all corners of the world to her family-owned property, thereby fulfilling her life-long dream of creating a world-class botanical garden. Nowadays, the property is administered by the National Trust; the adjoining terraced café and one of the Best of Barbados shops also belong to the estate. The shop has a very good selection of books about the flora & fauna of Barbados, as well as about the island's fascinating history. A leaflet given out at the entrance helps to identify the most important plants. *Daily 9 am–5 pm, admission 12 Bds$, Tel. 433 93 84, Bathsheba*

## Codrington College (105/D4)

An avenue lined with stately cabbage palms slopes gently to the college. Its founder, Christopher Codrington (1668–1710), belonged to one of the most distinguished planters' families of the island. After completing his college studies in England, he served the interests of the British crown in the Antilles as a diplomat and soldier. Upon his death, he be-

queathed his plantation house to a religious community. From the four wings that had been originally planned for the structure, only the southern wing was completed in 1743. Two years later it opened its doors as a primary school for the island's small elite. Since about 1830 the house has functioned as a college, exactly what Codrington intended it to be. Currently, the house is used by the University of the West Indies and the Theology Faculty of the Anglican Church of the West Indies. The chapel and the hall can be visited *daily from 1 pm to 4 pm.* Apart from the pretty structure made of coral stone, a stroll in the adjacent park is well worth your time. Next to the magnificent trees by the pond, a didactic nature trail takes visitors to a wilder part of the park. *St John*

## Ragged Point (105/F5)

At the eastern end of the island, where the strong waves of the Atlantic meet the placid waters of the Caribbean, a lone lighthouse keeps watch on this sunburnt stretch of coastline. From this vantage point, one can almost see the entire eastern coastline all the way to the *Pico Teneriffe* in the north. Ragged Point is a pretty and quiet little spot from which the beauty of this rugged coast can be appreciated. *The last part of the road soon becomes a dirt road. St Philip*

## St John's Church (104/C4)

The parish church of St John lies picturesquely at the end of the Hackleton Cliff high above the coast. The structure as it is seen today was completed in 1836 and is the Bajan version of the Anglican-Neogotic style. The very beauti-

*Exotic, delicate, valuable: the anthuriums of Tropical Blooms*

ful pulpit, heavily ornamented with wood carvings, was finished in 1876 and four local as well as two imported types of wood were used. The adjacent old cemetery has many characteristic family vaults, whose entrances are already half buried; only their roofs are seen above the ground. The church is one of the most visited sights on the island. *St John, at the end of Highway 3b*

### Tropical Blooms (103/F3)

In the hilly hinterland between Horse Hill and the Scotland District lies a very unusual botanical sight: the anthurium farm of Tom Hinds. Not easy to find, it is reached following Highway 3 towards Bathsheba, then when reaching Horse Hill near the police one turns to the left into Suriname Road. This narrow road takes visitors downhill to the farm. Even before entering the farm, the views from the road alone are worth the trip: miles and miles of palm groves and green meadows extend from here to the east coast. In the farm there are countless exotic anthuriums (also known as flamingo flowers) originally brought from their South American homeland in the Andes mountains to this tropical island. The plants grow under giant nets, never touching the ground. This very sensitive and highly domesticated variety of flamingo flower grows on coconut shells wrapped in plastic so they don't touch the soil. The heart of every amateur horticulturist beats faster upon seeing the unbelievable quantity of 25,000 plants showing off their 30,000 to 40,000 red, white and green flowers. Tom Hinds will gladly inform visitors about the difficult cultivation of this exotic but very beautiful species. The flowers from his farm can be bought in the departure lounge of the airport, after passing the customs and passport clearance. They are especially packaged and ready to be taken. (However, you should first find out whether you are allowed to introduce plants from abroad into your country.) *The shop is open daily from 7 am to 10 am and from 1.30 pm until 8 pm. The farm can only be visited by appointment, call first. Suriname, St Joseph, Tel. 433 13 00*

## RESTAURANTS

### Atlantis                          (104/B3)

❧ Once upon a time, the Atlantis was the place to go. This was long ago. Nowadays, the restaurant is still worth a visit, if only for the Sunday buffet. Exactly at 1 pm, the buffet featuring all of the island's specialities opens. For the main course, you can choose from two types of fish or chicken served with rice and a large selection of other tasty side dishes. If you are very hungry, you should fill your plate to the brim (!), as a second attempt to do so will meet with the stern glances of the strict ladies standing behind the pots. The loyal clientele consists mostly of middle-aged and older Barbadians, who have been coming here for years. The coconut cake is widely regarded as the island's best. The atmosphere resembles that of a lounge rather than that of a restaurant, but remember that nonetheless this is a Barbadian institution. When you make the reservation (by all means necessary!) you should ask for a table under the roofed terrace, as the view down to the fishing boats in Tent Bay is very romantic. During the week, the restaurant serves plain Barbadian fare. Reservations are also necessary in the evenings. *Daily 11 am–3 pm, 6.30 pm–*

*The powerful waves in the Soup Bowl challenge the best surfers*

*7.30 pm, Tent Bay, Bathsheba, St Joseph, Tel. 433 94 45, category 3*

## Barclays Park     (103/F1)

❀ This is a preferred picnic spot on weekends, when bajans come to this small restaurant mostly to purchase their beverages. It's a pity, since the *flying fish sandwich* is outstanding. At lunch-time, local dishes such as *beef stew, macaroni pie* and many others are served. However, sandwiches can be had at any time of the day. The pretty, white terrace offers a good view of the sea and of the hustle and bustle underneath. On Saturdays and Sundays, tour buses bring many locals in search of relaxation to this pretty beach. While some play, others sit around the wooden tables enjoying the food and beverages they have brought with them while they chat with the neighbours and even sample their food as well. *Daily 9.30 am–6.30 pm, longer on weekends, lunch from 11.30 am–3.30 pm, East Coast Rd., St Andrew, Tel. 433 56 14, category 3*

## Bonito Bar     (104/A-B3)

This is one of the favourite lunch destinations of the day-tour companies. Although the view of the rocky needles of Bathsheba is quite impressive, it has to be admired from the windows, as the restaurant lacks a terrace. *Daily 10 am–6 pm, Wed, Sun 1 pm–3 pm buffet, Bathsheba, St Joseph, Tel. 433 90 34, category 3*

## Edgewater Inn     (104/A3)

❧ The large dining room with its heavy mahogany furniture, walled sitting corners, dark wooden ceiling and leaded windows will remind anyone of a medieval castle in far away Europe. From the terrace full of nooks and crannies, however, guests will see an unforgettably beautiful view of the coast and the green hills of the Scotland District. A buffet is offered at noon on weekdays, and on Sundays a substantial brunch buffet. *Daily 7.30 am–9 pm, lunch buffet noon– 2.30 pm, Sun brunch buffet 12.30 pm–3 pm, Bathsheba, St Joseph, Tel. 433 99 00, category 2-3*

## Round House     (104/A-B3)

★ Several years ago, some Americans came to this rugged part of the island and fell in love with it instantly. They decided to open a restaurant in sleepy Bathsheba, bringing some life into this picturesque little village. It is possible to drop in in the evenings without reservation and try the delicious pizzas, pasta dishes and other Italian specialities served here. To accompany the meal, there is a salad served with truly American *blue cheese dressing*. The Round House is an old, renovated villa built on a slope and boasting a fantastic view of the palm groves, the coast and the turquoise sea. In the daytime, the small terrace is the ideal place to try the delicious rum punch served with tasty *flying fish sandwiches* and six different *dips*. In the evenings, guests dine in the brightly illuminated dining room. There is live music every Saturday night and Sunday afternoon. *Mon-Sat 8 am–10 pm, Sun 8 am–4 pm, Bathsheba, St Joseph, Tel. 433 96 78, category 2-3*

## Chalkey Mount Potteries   (103/E2)

High above, on top of the hills of the Scotland District, lies this potters' town. The pottery has traditional shapes and subdued colours; although the monkey-shaped jugs for the cool storage of drinking water are pretty and very original souvenirs. Visitors can watch the able hands of the potters as they mold their wares. To reach Chalkey Mount from Belleplaine, take Highway 2 towards Harrison's Cave/Welchman Hall Gully, after a good two kilometres take the narrow road to Chalkey Mount (signposted). *Mon–Sat 7.30 am–5.30 pm, somewhat shorter opening hours on Sun, Chalkey Mount, St Andrew*

### John C. Mayers Batik Gallery (104/A-B3)

The young artist John Mayers has achieved a good reputation in Barbados with his Indonesian batik creations. His works can also be purchased in some galleries, but it is far better to see how the artist works in his studio, a comfortable *chattel house* built on a slope of Bathsheba. He will gladly sell you his pretty creations featuring Barbadian motifs. *Daily 8 am–4 pm, Bathsheba, Cleavers Hill, St Joseph*

Accommodations are limited on the island's east coast. Since swimming in the ocean is often not possible, most tourists come to this part of the island on a day tour and very few of them stay overnight, except for some very bold surfers who are able to ride the dangerously high waves. However, you should not miss the beauty of the scenery and the magical soft dusk or dawn light of the coast near Bathsheba.

### Edgewater Inn (104/A3)

The hotel towers above the rugged coast battered by the heavy surf. It was built in the 1880's and was converted to a hotel about 1930. The rooms are very spacious, especially the suites lying above the cliffs (numbers 218 to 221). The heavy mahogany furniture and new radios with the old look fit perfectly well into the traditional atmosphere of the hotel. Guests feel they have been transported back in time, although the hotel

*Too dangerous for swimming, but ideal for walking along the beach – Cattlewash Bay*

still needs to catch up to new standards. For example, only recently have telephones been installed in every room and only two rooms have a balcony with a view of the sea: rooms 221 and especially 218, called 'the room with a view'. From this last room, guests can enjoy a fantastic double view of the rugged eastern and northern coastlines. The relative isolation of the Edgewater Inn should remind some guests of Thomas Mann's famous novel 'The Magic Mountain'. *20 rooms, Bathsheba, St Joseph, Tel. 433 99 00, Fax 433 99 02, www.edgewater-inn.com, category 2*

### Round House (104/A-B3)
This restaurant offers small but originally furnished rooms with wonderful views from upstairs. The roof terrace is the ideal place to relax and daydream. *4 rooms, Bathsheba, St Joseph, Tel. 433 96 78, Fax 433 90 79, www.funbarbados.com, category 2–3*

### Sea-U (104/B3)
★ The new pension was built in the colonial style and is entirely made of wood. It features large balconies surrounding the structure. The studio flats are spacious and have a kitchenette. They are surrounded by a large tropical garden and the ocean can be seen over the treetops. The heavy surf crashing against the rocks is a fascinating spectacle. The beach is only a few minutes away. Breakfast and dinner can be ordered. Under German management. *5 rooms, Tent Bay, Bathseba, St Joseph, Tel. 433 94 50, Fax 433 92 10, www.funbarbados.com, e-mail sea-u@caribsurf.com, category 2–3*

### Horseback riding (103/F3)
*Caribbean International Riding,* Ridings into the countryside by appointment, *Auburn Farm, near Highway 3, St Joseph, Tel. 433 14 53*

### Surfing (104/A-B2)
In the *Soup Bowl,* the powerful Atlantic waves reach the shore. Only the boldest surfers see the mighty waves more as a challenge than a life-threatening risk. Here and there, a few locals are seen with a surfboard under the arms; they will be glad to give advice. Surfboards can be hired at the *Bajan Surf Bungalow, Tel. 433 92 78* or at *Smoky's* opposite the Soup Bowl.

### Bath Recreation Park (105/D4)
★ The southernmost of the east coast beaches is also the only one where you can swim at all times. Under the bright shade of the casuarinas (also known as she-oaks or Australian pines), there are many picnic tables, mostly deserted during the week and ready to accommodate the weekend masses. The park is open *daily 10 am–5 pm, on weekends it opens at 9 am until dusk*

### Cattlewash Bay (104/A2)
★ An endless sandy beach starts north of Bathsheba. It is very beautiful but the corals and treacherous currents prevent one from swimming too deeply into the sea. The beach starts in Cattlewash, where several beach houses line its edges; farther on, the extensive unspoiled beach begins – until one reaches Barklays Park and continues into Belle-

plain. In the background, the bizarre rock formations and the rounded hilltops of the Scotland District make this a paradise for beach hikers and combers.

# SPEIGHTSTOWN AND THE NORTH

(**100/101**) Speightstown (pop. approx. 11,300) is, after Bridgetown, the second largest city on the island. From here, buses take passengers to the smallest settlements scattered on the northern end of the island and to Bathsheba in the east. Speightstown is a small but lively city that supplies the inhabitants of northern Barbados with their most essential needs. The city has no tourist attractions, yet a stroll through the typical, narrow and winding streets whilst passing many picturesque old houses is a lot of fun. If you follow the main street towards the ocean, you will soon reach the most famous restaurant-bar in all Barbados, the *Fisherman's Pub* – the perfect place to enjoy a romantic Caribbean sunset.

Highway 1 runs behind the settlement of (**100/B4-5**) *Mile and a Quarter* (in case anyone hadn't guessed it – the village is located exactly 1.25 miles away from Speightstown) and is reached by driving through various interesting cultivated fields. The decapitated towers of the sugar mills and the abandoned factories bear witness to those times when sugar was still king. The road then goes slightly uphill and comes to an enchanted mahogany forest. The high, curved treetops above the road resemble a cathedral ceiling. As one drives past the thick bushes

and the aerial roots of other tropical trees, one almost gets the impression of crossing a primeval tropical rain forest. As soon as the highest point of (**101/D4**) *Cherry Hill* is reached, the forest suddenly ends – ✥ and the east coast is seen down below. Now the winding road starts going steeply downhill; palms and cattle pastures are seen left and right. New vistas of the rugged coast and the hills of the Scotland District open up after every curve, one more impressive than the other. Shortly before the end of what is probably the most impressive drive on the island, one sees the white sails of the large *Morgan Lewis Mill*, the sugar mill museum.

## SIGHTS

### Arbib Nature & Heritage Trail                    (100/A5)

Guided hikes through gorges and sugar cane plantations are a wonderful opportunity to get to know rural Barbados. Hikers have the choice of two different trails, a short or a long one. *Wed, Thurs and Sat 2.30 pm, advanced booking obligatory, admission 15 Bds$, Speights-town, St Peter, Tel. 426 24 21*

### Barbados Wildlife Reserve/ Grenade Hall Forest & Signal Station         (101/D4-5)

This wildlife reserve situated in the middle of a mahogany forest was opened to the public in 1985. The narrow, winding road paved with the bricks of the former sugar factory takes visitors to the different parts of the park, which isn't very big. There are monkeys (the Barbados green monkeys), deer, flamingos, otters, snakes, turtles, fish, a small crocodile and some other animals. There are also several macaws in the birdhouse, although some of them are housed in smaller cages. The visit to the park may be recommended for families, but the overall impression not a very favourable one, even somewhat depressing. The price of admission includes the visit to the Grenade Signal Station and the 2-km-long didactic nature trail in the forest, a few steps above the Wild Life Reserve itself. The former ruins of the Signal Station were completely renovated. With the help of a recorded tour, tourists learn the most interesting facts about these typical Barbadian towers. The photos and written information supplement the historical digression. Downstairs, the display cases show some archaeological finds. *Daily 10 am–5 pm, admission 23 Bds$, Farley Hill, on Highway 2, St Peter*

Belafonte and Joan Fontaine were shot here, although it was supposed to be Jamaica. This was once the most elegant plantation house in the whole island; sadly, it is now reduced to a ghost of its former self after a large fire destroyed it. Only the façade remains. Even the ruins give a good impression of its former glory; they would make a good set for a Hitchcock movie. The park is still lovely – an oasis of tranquillity, especially in the cool early morning hours when only the chirping of the numerous birds interrupts the silence. Benches invite strollers to take a break in the half shade and read or maybe admire the view of the east coast and the endless sugar canes as they are moved by the breeze. There is a playground for the children, too. *Daily 8.30 am–6 pm, admission 3 Bds$ per vehicle, brochure 2 Bds$, on Highway 2, St Peter*

### Farley Hill National Park  (100/C5)

★ ⬙ A while back, some exteriors of the Hollywood classic 'Island in the Sun' starring Harry

### Morgan Lewis Mill  (101/E4)

⬙ This sugar mill, the best preserved of all, would be fully operational if its wings were still fitted

*Farley Hill, one of the film sets for 'Island in the Sun'*

*Morgan Lewis Mill, the only completely preserved sugar mill*

with sails. For over two centuries, these mills characterized the landscape of most Caribbean islands where the main cash crop was sugar. Until 1947 the mill pressed the precious sweet juice from the plants. A small exhibit is housed inside the mill. The view from the top towards the east coast is a good reason to climb the stairs. *Mon–Fri 9 am–5 pm, admission 10 Bds$, in the southern part of Cherry Tree Hill, St Andrew*

### St Nicholas Abbey (101/D4)

The plantation built in the Jacobean style is almost unique. There are only two others built in this architectural style on the whole continent. The structure was built between 1650 and 1660. The fireplaces with their distinctive chimneys found in the upper floor were not needed in the tropical Caribbean climate, of course, but since the blueprints came directly from England it was decided to go ahead and build them. The beautiful wood panelling in the large living rooms dates back to 1898 and some of the furniture is even from the 18th century; the English porcelain from the early 19th century. The plantation has existed since 1640. Why it was called an abbey remains a mystery. Only the ground floor is open to the public, as the property is still owned by the family. *Mon–Fri 10 am–3.30 pm, admission 5 Bds$, St Peter*

## RESTAURANTS

### Fish frying stall (100/A5)

❀ A simple stand with a charcoal grill, a couple of pots, plenty of prepared fish fillets, a large refrigerator full of cold beverages – those are the only ingredients for creating a fast and nutritious meal complete with side dishes. Everything is served on plastic plates and eaten while sitting on a wooden bench or under a tree. *Fri from 6 pm, Sat all day, Road View, south of Speightstown, St Peter, beside the Sandridge Hotel, category 3*

### Fisherman's Pub                (100/A5)

✹ The modest restaurant with the ever changing daily menu is more a pub than a restaurant and easily the most popular place in Speightstown on weekends. There is a large terrace with a view of the ocean. *Daily 8 am– midnight, Fri, Sat stays open later, Speightstown, St Peter, Tel. 422 27 03, category 3*

### Mango's by the Sea            (100/A5)

★ The cosy restaurant with the large veranda covered by palm fans and hanging porcelain lamps is located in the centre of Speightstown and by the sea. Fresh fish is served daily, and once a week there is *lobster night*. Don't forget the vegetarian spaghetti, the ribs and especially the delicious cheese cake. Service is friendly and efficient, too. A small gallery is part of the restaurant. Shuttle service on request. The cigar bar opens at 10 pm. *Sun–Fri 6 pm– 9.30 pm, West End, 2 Queen Street, Speightstown, St Peter, Tel. 422 07 04, category 1–2*

### Mullins                        (108/A6)

Popular beach restaurant directly on Mullins Bay beach. *Daily 8.30 am until the late evening hours, Mullins Bay, St Peter, Tel. 422 18 78, category 2–3*

## HOTELS

Immediately south of Speightstown there is a good selection of hotels, whereas to the north there are only the two hotels listed here:

### Almond Beach Village         (100/A5)

North of Speightstown, the island's largest hotel complex can be seen. Located on the long beach in Six Men's Bay, there's even a golf course. All rooms, though not spacious, have a TV and a balcony and form part of individual two-storeyed buildings. For those with wedding plans, the hotel even takes care of the necessary arrangements. The old sugar mill or the beach pavilion is ideally suited for the purpose. The Almond Beach Village and its smaller associated hotel appropriately named *Almond Beach Club* on the west coast are all-inclusive, top-rated hotels. There is live entertainment every evening; in addition, sports facilities for tennis, fitness training, sauna, gymnastics, golf, water skiing, surfing, snorkelling and banana boating are offered to the guests free of charge. The holiday village boasts nine pools and is ideal for families. The so-called *dine-around programmes* make it possible to dine in other restaurants of the west coast. *288 rooms, Speightstown, St Peter, Tel. 422 49 00, Fax 422 06 17, category 1 (all-inclusive)*

### Cobblers Cove                 (100/A6)

The centre of this elegant hotel complex consisting of two-storeyed buildings with gabled roofs built in the English country house style is the splendid villa

*At the Almond Beach Village, all wishes come true*

which houses the lobby and library. All rooms are furnished with rattan furniture and have a kitchenette. The large terraces offer a wonderful view of the sea. Tennis and water sports are included; in the winter the hotel can only be booked with half-board. Children under 12 are not admitted between mid-January and mid-March. The resort is a member of the Relais & Château hotel group. *40 suites, St Peter, Tel. 422 22 91, Fax 422 14 60, www.barbados.org, category 1*

### Kings Beach (100/A5)

The beach with its fine sand and gorgeous palms looks idyllic. The two-storeyed hotel built in the Spanish style opens up halfway towards the beach and is under Swiss management. It is very popular with European holiday-makers booking package tours. *57 rooms, Road View, St Peter, Tel. 422 16 90, Fax 422 16 91, www. barbados.org, category 1*

### Legend Garden (100/A6)

Nicely hidden away directly opposite Mullins beach, this small family-run hotel lies in the middle of a garden. The flats are attractively painted in many different colours. Pool. *8 studio apartments, Mullins Bay, St Peter, Tel. 422 43 69, Fax 422 20 56, e-mail legendcondos@sunbeach.net, category 2–3*

### Sandridge Beach (100/A5)

One of the very few reasonably priced hotels directly on the beach. The three-storeyed building lies at an angle to the beach. A lagoon cuts off a sort of natural swimming pool; the beach in front of the hotel is narrow, but the meadow with sun-loungers is quite large. Most rooms come equipped with a kitchenette. *58 rooms, St Peter, Tel. 422 23 61, Fax 422 19 65, category 2*

### Sugar Cane Club (100/B4-5)

Although the bungalows built in the Spanish hacienda style are not directly on the beach, they are nevertheless enchantingly situated inland and far away from the hustle and bustle. This is the island's northernmost hotel. Most of the one-storeyed bungalows have a terrace overlooking the large garden and have a small kitchen, a walled sitting corner and open gables. From the elevated swimming pool guests have a good view of the cultivated fields extending all the way to the ocean. The adjacent hotel restaurant offers a good selection of international dishes, from spaghetti and shish-kabobs to Wiener schnitzel. *(category 2-3)*. Free *shuttle service* to the beaches and the super market. *22 rooms, Maynards, St Peter, Tel. 422 50 26, Fax 422 05 22, category 2–3*

### Golf (100/A5)
The Almond Beach Village has its own, small 9-hole golf course par 3 on the hotel grounds themselves. Guests of the Village and of the associated hotel Almond Beach Club can use it free of charge. *Tel. 422 49 00*

### Beaches
❖ South of Speightstown, the wide and lively beach of (**100/A6**) *Mullins Bay* temptingly entices locals and tourists. The numerous pedlars and beachboys with the fast jet skis are seen commuting all the time between Mullins Bay and (**100/A5**) *Six Men's Bay* at the Almond Beach Village. The pretty beach with graceful palms growing to within a few feet of the ocean as well as with poisonous *manchineel trees* is used almost exclusively by the hotel guests. A marina is being built to the immediate north. We can only hope that the beach is not going to suffer because of it.

### Water sports
All hotels offer the typical water sports, and those on Mullins Bay are no exception.

## ENTERTAINMENT

### Chattel Bar (100/A5)
The bar in the new *chattel house* is not only the favourite meeting place of the guests of the Sandridge Beach Hotel in the evenings, but it is also owned by it. In the relaxed, cosy atmosphere, the drinks taste better than ever. *Daily 10.30 am–midnight, opposite the Sandridge Hotel*

### Fisherman's Pub (100/A5)
On weekends, this is the most frequented place for Speightstowners.

---

#### Rum punch

A rhyme helps you prepare a cocktail the traditional way: 'one-sour (lemon juice), two-sweet (sugar syrup), three-strong (rum), four-weak (water and ice)', then a dash of Angostura bitter and before serving sprinkle a pinch of nutmeg.

For Bajans, a *rum punch* is not something you drink every day, but is reserved for special occasions like picnics. Punch has a long tradition; it was already drunk in early colonial times. It is believed that the largest punch bowl is the creation of Christopher Codrington. The bowl is made of richly ornamented silver and has a diameter of 45.7 cm. In the 18th century, a funeral without the consumption of generous quantities of punch was simply inconceivable.

# Unspoiled bays and beaches

*These routes are marked in green on the map on the inside front cover and in the Road Atlas beginning on page 100*

## ① TO THE UNSPOILED BAYS AND BEACHES

 **Following the eastern coastline from Bathsheba, you drive southwards until you reach the Crane Beach Hotel on the south-east coast. The roughly 30-km-drive takes you to isolated villages, picturesque bays and empty beaches. Depending on how many breaks you need, the drive can take from half a day to a full day. Those in a hurry can combine this tour with the route 'Through the Middle' described below.**

You leave *Andromeda Botanic Gardens* (p. 71) in Bathsheba and take a southern course as you start driving up the hills. At the first fork, you turn sharply to the left and continue driving on the narrow, winding East Coast Road. Tall, graceful coconut palms line both sides of the road. Soon you reach a plantation, easily recognized by the characteristic conical tower of its old sugar mill. After a while, the coconut palms give way to banana plantations – a sign that you are now in the St John parish, where most of the sweet, yellow fruit is cultivated. Although the coast remains visible from the road, you will have to take one of the side roads if you wish to reach the sea so you can take a break swimming in a cove or walking along the beach.

After three kilometres, a detour forces drivers to pass through a small settlement. The winding road lengthens the journey, but the main road was undermined and washed away years ago and there are no plans to rebuild it. Although in some ways the cultivation of bananas is a blessing because it has brought prosperity to the region, in other ways it has been a disaster. The original forest was cut down, so the typically heavy downpours of the summer and early fall rain season can be very destructive as the enormous quantities of water rapidly flow downhill to reach the ocean. Many roads and tracks become fast-flowing rivers, thereby undermining and destroying the pavement. In order to prevent the damage, wire containers are filled with the more resistant coral debris. The resulting 'building stones' are placed underneath the pavement, thus giving the whole pavement a more secure hold than the loose rock underneath the pavement would provide.

You drive past a chicken farm, a primary school, then past the disproportionately large village church. When you once again see the ruins of another old sugar mill you are back to the main road. Soon, you turn to the left to reach *St Martins Bay*. The road leads directly to the sea. People take out their cushions and pillows to air them. Down below, the breaking waves almost reach the foundations of the houses. Few people are seen here. Everything gives the impression of being more or less abandoned, making this the ideal place for those in search of melancholic isolation.

The road continues in a curve and climbs sharply. A small supermarket is seen on the left, at the intersection with the main street. You turn to the left and keep driving southwards. You see the numerous spear-shaped purple lilies shooting up into the air; the yellowish croton bushes and the bright red flowers of the poinsettias make this a delightful drive through the colourful countryside. Then, the scenery changes; everything seems to open up as the fields and meadows become wider. The ruins of yet another sugar factory point the way to the *Bath Recreation Park* (p. 77). A dense field of sugar cane prevents you from seeing a beautiful, protected lagoon until you almost stumble into it. This is the only place on the eastern coast where it is almost always possible to swim.

Back to the main road, treacherous waves in the asphalt force drivers to watch out. Once you have drastically reduced your driv-

ing speed and become used to the waves, these are easily mastered. After 10 km, a road to the right leads to *St John's Church* (p. 72). You must stop here and get off; not only is the little parish church worth visiting, but its unique location high above the coast is a truly unforgettable sight.

You continue on a southern course and soon drive past a lively village by the roadside. Then you turn into a shady avenue. To your right, you see the beautiful access road leading to *Codrington College* (p. 72) bordered by graceful palms. Soon thereafter, you turn to the left and reach Consett Bay. The road turns to the right and shortly afterwards you have to turn to the left once again or else you will come back to the main street. The deserted little road winds its way through thick low bushes until it suddenly reaches the coast. Quite unexpectedly, you are in a wide bay; numerous colourful fishing boats rest on the beach. A narrow foot-bridge projects into the placid lagoon protected from the powerful ocean currents by off-shore reefs. Only a few holiday houses are seen on the hillside; otherwise, you have the feeling that you have reached the end of the world.

Soon thereafter, the road swerves before reaching a pink house with a small corner shop. This is the place to stop for a drink or bite. The little shop itself is worth looking at. It is chock-full of every possible article needed for everyday life on Barbados, from fabric to nail polish. The friendly elderly lady proudly presides over her domain.

Just one last downhill journey: at the park with its pretty picnic benches turn left, then you have reached the flat southern lowlands. At km 19 turn sharply to the left towards Highway 5. In front of you, the rusty lighthouse of *Ragged Point* (p. 72) can be discerned. From now on, the road continues through a uniformly populated region. Opposite a newly built district, an inconspicuous sign shows the fork leading to *Bottom Bay* (p. 53). It's hard to believe that such an inconspicuous access road leads to an unbelievably spectacular beach! When you continue, remember to turn to the left at the stop sign of km 25. A sign shows the way to Crane via Sam Lord's Castle. At the next stop sign, the left cul-de-sac takes visitors to the *Sam Lord's Castle* (p. 52) hotel. Remember to stay on your right in order to turn to the left at the next stop sign. When the road turns sharply to the right, you have reached the back access road to *Crane Beach* (p. 52).

In case you haven't yet swum in Bath or in Bottom Bay, you should by all means do so now in the long, inviting surf of Crane Beach. Afterwards, rest your tired extremities on the powdery pink-white sand and relax while you enjoy the beautiful blue sky and watch the white fluffy cumulus clouds blown by the trade winds passing over your head. This is paradise indeed if there ever was one!

## ② THROUGH THE MIDDLE

 **The winding paths of this tour take you from the gentle west coast to the wild and romantic Atlantic coast. The drive provides good glimpses of village life; the fantastic views will more than compensate for the difficult and tiresome stretches of road that this journey to the countryside requires. The 25 km can be covered in two hours without breaks.**

In Holetown, turn towards the interior as soon as you see the small church in front of the First Avenue. The road climbs steadily as you drive past villas and *chattel houses* at the large roundabout, cross Highway 2 a and leave the white St Thomas Parish Church to your right behind you. The road keeps climbing the hills. In the next fork, remain to your right. Casuarinas and sugar cane grow all the way to the edge of the road. At the stop sign, continue driving straight ahead; soon, you will be driving through a green and shady passage spanned by a wide arch. Behind it, impressive cabbage palms line the road. At the next stop sign you turn to the left – you have finally reached the island's back. The endless view of sugar cane moved by the wind reaches as far as the horizon; in the distance, you can see the numerous telecommunica-tions antennas on top of *Mount Misery* (p. 57), which at 328 m, is the island's second-highest mountain.

For a while, follow the signs showing the way to the Flower Forest. On the right side, the sugar cane fields give way to cotton fields. Close to harvest time, you can see the myriad white dots of the opened seed husks. Later, the fields give way to pastureland and after 5 km you come to the *Highland Outdoor Center.* Shortly thereafter, the road narrows and begins its downhill course. Although this stretch of road demands the full concentration of the driver, you should not miss the first view down into the east coast. You pass the lower entrance to the *Welchman Hall Gully* (p. 59) to the right. If you have time and energy, you may want to stretch your legs and take a walk through this impressive earth fracture. The interesting walk through the narrow gorge takes only about half an hour.

At the next stop sign, continue driving straight ahead for a short time, then turn to the left. At the corner you will see an exotic wooden house, where Rastafarians sell vegetables. At km 7, a narrow road branches off to the *Flower Forest*. The botanical garden occupies a large expanse of land; apart from the numerous interesting tropical flowers, the stunning view is the other attraction of this place *(daily 9 am–5 pm, admission Bds$ 13.80)*.

As you drive on, keep to the right and when you come to the next fork, turn left. Ignore the next fork and continue on the road as it starts going downhill. The vegetation becomes increasingly lush; soon, breadfruit trees envelop the road. The dark blue expanse of the Atlantic is now seen in front of you. At km 9, the road once again branches off in two directions, remain to the left. The *Scotland District* (p. 78) is now at your feet – on the left you will recognize the deep green hues of the *Turners Hall Wood*, one of the last remaining untouched forests on the island.

At the next fork, you will notice that the left road leading downhill is closed, so take the right one going uphill and follow the sign to Chalky Mount. When you reach the top, turn to the left; in the next intersection make sure to remain on the left side of the road. Drive past a white wall, then continue on the left side of the road.

Those who would like to visit a picturesque village should take a detour to the right, which leads to *Cambridge*. Return the same way, as the road ends there. The next village is *Chalky Mount* – to reach the pottery workshop, turn to the right at the school (p. 27). Straight ahead, the road goes downhill; soon, fruit trees line both sides of the road. You have reached the most intensively cultivated part of the island. The sour, vitamin-rich Barbadian cherry grows profusely on the branches of the small, bush-like trees.

At km 17, you reach the petrol station of Belleplaine. This is the only chance you will have to fill up because it is the only petrol station in the whole east coast. At the small roundabout, turn right into the Erny Bourne Highway, which the people keep calling by its other name of East Coast Highway. The road continues directly along the coast; the prevailing strong winds have bent the coastal vegetation. After passing some dunes, a bizarre sandstone formation called 'The Sleeping Napoleon' and a couple of vacation homes, you have finally reached *Cattlewash* (p. 77). There is one more hill to climb, then you are at the intersection of Bathsheba where you can make up your mind whether you want to turn left and downhill to the Soup Bowl and see the bold surfers riding the powerful Atlantic waves or turn right to Bridgetown – about a 35-minute ride – or maybe follow the signs leading to the nearby Andromeda Botanic Gardens so you can combine this tour with the one described above that leads to the south.

# Practical information

*Important addresses and useful information
for your trip to Barbados*

## AMERICAN & BRITISH ENGLISH

Marco Polo travel guides are written in British English. In North America, certain terms and usages deviate from British usage. Some of the more frequently encountered examples are: *baggage for luggage, billion for milliard, cab for taxi, car rental for car hire, drugstore for chemist's, fall for autumn, first floor for groundfloor, freeway/highway for motorway, gas(oline) for petrol, railroad for railway, restroom for toilet/lavatory, streetcar for tram, subway for underground/tube, toll-free numbers for freephone numbers, trailer for caravan, trunk for boot, vacation for holiday, wait staff for waiting staff (in restaurants etc.), zip code for postal code.*

## BOAT TRIPS

Plenty of boat trips are offered, most of them with Bridgetown as the starting point for the trips along the west coast. You may choose to book a sailing ship tour instead; most take place on catamarans or on one of the larger pleasure ships. The boat trips offered are day tours starting at about 10 am and lasting until 2 pm or 3 pm. Those of the *Sunset Cruises* last until dusk. Some ships offer a romantic dinner tour in the evenings. A day trip including lunch costs about 100 Bds$ per person.

## BUSES

The island's most important traffic junction is the capital city of Bridgetown. From the *Fairchild Street Bus Terminal* located at the end of the Careenage, the big, blue country buses depart to the south and east approx. every half-hour. The buses going to the west and north depart from the *Lower Green Bus Terminal* situated at St Mary's Church to the west of the city centre. Near both of these bus terminals you will also find the private yellow minibuses as well as the *route taxis*. Those are *vans*, that take passengers mostly along the southern coast and have a capacity for 12. They may stop anywhere; be ready to stop the moment the driver sticks his hand out. The large buses stop only at the bus stops. *To City* means that they are going to Bridgetown, *Out of City* that they are coming from Bridgetown. It is also possible to stop a bus with a hand signal. The fare costs 1.50 Bds$ and it makes no difference which type of bus you ride. Remember that the blue buses give out no change. Important points for changing buses are Speightstown in the north and Oistins in the south. All buses run from 6 am until midnight.

## CLIMATE & WHEN TO GO

Because Barbados is in the tropics, the average maximum temperatures in the daytime are between 28 to 31 degrees centigrade (80 to 88 °F) with relatively low humidity levels. The temperature is constant throughout the year and the days are rarely warmer or cooler. A constant trade wind blows with a speed of 16 to 24 km/h, which greatly helps to cool down the daytime temperature. The average annual precipitation is 1,250 mm on the coast; at the island's highest point it is 1,650 mm. The sun shines more than 3,000 hours per year. The high season runs from mid-December to mid-April. During this season, all prices are significantly higher than those in the remaining months of the year. By all means visit the island during the low season if you can, as you will save money. But keep in mind that the rain season lasts from July to November, which coincides with the hurricane season as well.

## CONSULATES

On Barbados:
**Canadian High Commission**
*Bishop's Court Hill, Collymore Rock, St Michael, Barbados, Tel. 429 35 50, Fax 437 74 36*

**British High Commission**
*PO Box 676, Lower Collymore Rock, St Michael, Barbados, Tel. 436 66 94, Fax 430 78 60*

**Embassy of the United States of America**
*PO Box 302, Canadian Imperial Bank of Commerce Building; Broad Street, Bridgetown, Barbados, Tel. 436 49 50, Fax 429 52 46, e-mail clo@state.gov*

In Canada:
**Barbados High Commission**
*130 Albert Street, Suite 302, Ottawa, Ontario, K1P 5G4, Tel. (613) 236 95 17/8, Fax (613) 230 43 62, e-mail barhcott@travel-net.com*

In the U.K.:
**Barbados High Commission**
*1 Great Russell Street, London WC1B 3JY, Tel. (0171) 631 49 75, Fax (0171) 323 68 72, e-mail barcomuk@dial.pipex.com*

In the USA:
**Embassy of Barbados**
*2144 Wyoming Avenue, NW, Washington, DC 20008, Tel. (202) 923 92 00, Fax (202) 332 74 67, www.barbados.org, e-mail BARBADOS@oas.org*

## CURRENCY

Banks are only in Bridgetown, Holetown and Speightstown, but this is not too important for the average tourists quite simply because banks are not the only places where money can be exchanged; their rate is no better than what you get in other places. Banks open from *Mon–Thurs 8 am–3 pm, Fri 8 am–5 pm.* Every hotel changes foreign currency and travellers cheques; US$ are preferred. In the larger restaurants you can pay with travellers cheques in US$. All major credit cards are widely accepted. If you run out of Barbadian dollars, it is also possible to pay with US$.

But for the smaller restaurants, street traders, buses, etc. you should have Barbadian money in cash.

The Barbados dollar (Bds$) is worth approximately one-half US dollar. The official rate is 1.98 Bds$ for 1 US dollar. Other currencies are subject to the usual currency fluctuations. The banknotes in circulation are: 2, 5, 10, 20, 50 and 100 Bds$. The following coins are used: *one cent, five, ten, twenty-five cents* and *one dollar.*

## CUSTOMS

If you intend to shop in the numerous duty-free shops, then be prepared to show your passport and airplane ticket. If you don't want to carry these important documents with you wherever you go, then it's also possible to have the hotel reception certify the copies. But it is possible to make purchases without the documents, in which case the merchandise will be brought to the airport or harbour. This rule applies in all cases to wine and spirits as well as tobacco products.

If you are a resident of the EU, you may purchase souvenirs and other goods up to approx. US$ 180, 2 litres of wine and 2 additional litres of other alcoholic beverages with an alcohol content of up to 22% or 1 litre with an alcohol content of over 22%. Also, 200 cigarettes, 100 cigarillos, 50 cigars or 250g of tobacco. The following items may be taken into Barbados by persons aged 18 and over without customs duty: 200 cigarettes or 250 g tobacco; 750 ml of spirits and 750 ml of wine; 50 g of perfume; gifts up to a value of Bds$ 100. The following items are prohibited: foreign rum, fresh fruit and articles made of camouflaged material.

## DRIVING & CAR RENTAL

As in the U.K., people drive on the left. Once you get accustomed to this, you will notice that it isn't difficult to drive on the 'wrong' side of the road at all. Since the steering wheel in rented cars is always on the right side, it's only logical to drive on the left side of the street. However, avoid driving in Bridgetown's heavy traffic at first; it's possible to have the car rental companies bring you the vehicle to your hotel. Then, you can slowly get used to the unfamiliar driving conditions on an empty country road.

Barbados has a good and very extensive road network that spans (believe it or not) 1,280 km. The roads are generally well maintained and paved. A wide highway resembling a motorway connects the international airport with the capital and also partly encircles it before continuing on to the west coast. It's a quick drive unless you get stuck in rush-hour traffic. The maximum speed outside the city centre and in the outskirts of villages is 60 km/h; in the countryside 80 km/h is allowed for only short periods. Many intersections have *roundabouts* to regulate traffic flow. Keep in mind that the cars that are already in the roundabout have the right of way. Traffic lights are rare. When you see three lights next to each other, the left one is for those turning to the left, the middle one for traffic continuing straight ahead and the right light for those wishing to turn to the right. However, a Bajan driver prefers to indicate a turn not by blinking but by sticking out his hand instead. Stop signs are found on both sides of an inter-section. The car that arrives first is the one that has the right of way. Watch out for the numerous buses, as they may stop without warning.

The most popular type of rented car is the *Moke*. Generally, these small vehicles lack any doors and have a collapsible roof instead. They are ideal for relaxed driving all through Barbados. There is a good selection of cars for rent. Tourists are granted a national driving permit by showing their driving license and paying 10 Bds$, to be paid in cash. The corresponding car rental company issues them. Two recommended companies are: *Sunny Isle Motors, Worthing Main Rd., Christ Church, Tel. 435 79 79, Fax 43 59 2 77, e-mail sunisle@carib surf.com* and *Courtesy Rent-a-Car,* the only company represented at the airport (with three additional branches on the island) *Tel. 431 41 60, Fax 429 63 87, e-mail courtesy@ Goddent.com.*

## EMERGENCIES

Police, *Tel. 211*
Fire, *Tel. 311*
Ambulance, *Tel. 511*

## HEALTH & DRINKING WATER

Tap water, which is 96% ground water, is safe. This is due to the fact that the geological composition of the island is relatively uniform, consisting of limestone and coral. These layers act as outstanding filters, with the result that few chemicals are needed to purify the water. Generally speaking, Barbadians are very healthy people and the average life expectancy is 70.5 years, a well documented fact. The main hospital is the *Queen Elizabeth Hospital (Tel. 435 64 50)* in Bridge-town. This is the place where most specialists are found, many of whom have studied in the USA or Canada. In addition, there are several other provincial hospitals as well as the private *Bay View Hospital* in St Michael *(Tel. 436 54 46).*

## ISLAND-HOPPING

### BWIA
The Trinidad/Tobago airline flies from Barbados to the neighbouring islands of Antigua, Grenada, Jamaica, St Maarten, Trinidad/Tobago and to Guyana and Caracas/Venezuela in South America. *Sunjet House, Bridgetown, Tel. 426 21 11*

### Chantours
This company organizes day trips to the Grenadines. *Plaza 2, Sunset Crest, St James, Tel. 432 55 91, Fax 432 55 40, www. chantours.com*

### Grenadine Tours
A day trip includes a visit to Mustique and the Grenadines or Union Island, Mayreau, Tobago Cays, Mopion or Palm Island can also be visited. *27 Hastings Plaza, Hastings, Christ Church, Tel. 435 84 51, Fax 435 64 44, www. barbados. org/tours*

### LIAT
The Caribbean airline based in St Lucia flies from Barbados to Antigua, the Dominican Republic, Grenada, Guyana, St Lucia, St Vincent, Trinidad and Tobago, among other places. Several day passes make 'island-hopping' possible. *St Michael's Plaza, Bridgetown, Tel. 434 54 28; airport office Tel. 428 09 8*

### Mustique Airways
Daily flights to the Grenadines as well as to St Vincent, Bequia, Mustique, Canouan and Union Is-

land. *27 Hastings Plaza, Tel. 435 7009, at the airport: Tel. 428 16 38*

## Windward Lines

The M. V. 'Windward' is a large and modern, 60-m-long ferry with a maximum capacity for 250 passengers. It provides service from Barbados to Venezuela and back. The week-long-trip stops for several hours in St Lucia, St Vincent, Trinidad and Margarita. There are cabins for approx. 70 passengers. The 'Windward' is no luxurious transatlantic, so the fare is much more reasonable. *7 James Fort Building, Hincks Str., Tel. 431 04 49, e-mail windward@sjds.net*

This ambitious project under construction is called Port St Charles. The yachts, though, are already anchored in the unfinished harbour and their owners have already moved into their exclusive villas. *St Peter, Tel. 419 10 00, Fax 422 46 46,e-mail reservations@portstcharles.com.bb*

## MARRIAGE

In order to marry in Barbados, you need a valid passport or the original birth certificate or a copy there of certified by a notary public as well as a return flight ticket. The fee is 52.50 US$. Marriage candidates must apply in person at the *Ministry of Home Affairs, General Post Office Building, Cheapside, Bridgetown, Mon–Fri 8.15 am–4.30 pm, Tel. 228 89 50, Fax 437 37 94*

## MEASURES & WEIGHTS

| | |
|---|---|
| 1 cm | 0.39 inches |
| 1 m | 1.09 yards (3.28 feet) |
| 1 km | 0.62 miles |
| 1 m² | 1.20 sq. yards |
| 1 ha | 2.47 acres |
| 1 km² | 0.39 sq. miles |
| 1 g | 0.035 ounces |
| 1 kg | 2.21 pounds |
| 1 British tonne | 1016 kg |
| 1 US ton | 907 kg |

*1 litre is equivalent to 0.22 Imperial gallons and 0.26 US gallons*

## NEWSPAPERS

The oldest daily newspaper in Barbados is the *Barbados Advocat,* founded in 1895. Since 1973, the more widely read *Nation* competes against it. Both newspapers publish Sunday editions and two specialized editions with tourist information. Other publications are *The Visitor*, published weekly, and the *Sunseeker*, published twice a month. The latter are free and can be obtained in hotels and restaurants. They publish information about current weekly events and articles dealing with holiday topics.

## PASSPORT & VISA

Visitors from the U.K. need a valid passport, those coming from the USA and Canada need either a valid passport or another official identification document and a ticket showing proof of return. The maximum stay allowed is six months. Every visitor gets an *Immigration Card* on the airplane, which has to be shown to the officer with the passport. The valid passport should still be valid for three additional months upon departure.

## PHOTOGRAPHY

Although Bajans are more tolerant than their neighbours when it comes to snapshots, ask for permission to photograph the person. If you do it courteously, you will probably get a positive response. In case you don't, as can be the case with older Bajans or those working in the fields, respect their wishes. Bring your own film, it is much cheaper in your home country than in Barbados.

## POST OFFICE

Leave your stamped postcards and letters at the hotel reception, the mail is picked up daily. Every parish has its own post office, the main post office is located in *Cheapside, Bridgetown, Tel. 436 48 00*

## SIGHTSEEING FLIGHTS

### Helicopter Tours
20- to 35-minute sightseeing flights over Barbados cost approx. 145 to 245 Bds$ per person. *The Bridgetown Heliport, Tel. 431 00 69*

## SKINNY-DIPPING & TOPLESS

Skinny-dipping and going topless is not permitted. This also applies to hotel swimming pools. Barbadians are very pious people and the local churches do not tolerate the public display of bare facts.

## SPORTS

Barbados is a typical Caribbean island offering endless possibilities for the water sports enthusiasts. Apart from that, there are quite a few golf courses.

### Golf
The island has four golf courses. *Royal Westmoreland, Sandy Lane, Rockley* and *Belair.*

### Deep-sea fishing
Those wishing to imitate Hemingway and undertake a deep-sea fishing tour should get together with others wanting to do the same and charter a boat or join a group. Well-known fishing tour companies: *Blue Marlin Charters, Tel. 436 43 22; Blue Jay, Tel. 422 20 98, Fax 435 66 55*

### Jogging
During the first weekend in December, the famous *Run Barbados International Road Race Series* including a marathon and a ten-kilometre-run take place on the island.

### Horse races
The *Garrison Savannah* racetrack located in the outskirts of Bridgetown opens from January to April and from August to November. The exact dates are published in the Barbadian newspapers. The Barbadians love horse races as much as the British, the betting even more. *Barbados Turf Club, Tel. 426 39 80*

### Horseback riding
The hilly hinterland and the wide expanses of fields are ideal for horseback riding. Organized tours, even for greenhorns, are offered by *Highland Outdoor Tours (Canefield, St Thomas, Tel. 438 80 69).*

### Surfing
The best time for wind surfing is from December to March – the thermal winds provide surfers with excellent conditions. The southern coast with its strong winds and high waves is preferred by advanced surfers, while the western coast is ideal for beginners. Most hotels rent boards, some even provide them free of charge. On the east coast, the high Atlantic waves have

been luring the daring wave riders for years. Their favourite meeting place is Bathsheba.

## Diving

Although the coral reefs of the southern and western coasts are not the best of the Caribbean, they are still good enough for the experienced diver and for those wanting to become one. By all means dive down into the depths to marvel at the beauty of the colourful tropical underwater world. Many diving schools offer their services.

## Tennis

Many hotels have lighted tennis courts. There are public tennis courts in Folkestone Park in Holetown on the west coast.

## Hiking

Every *Sun at about 6 am* and in the afternoons at *3.30 pm* free guided hiking tours are offered. Further information at: *Barbados National Trust, Tel. 426 24 21 and 436 90 33.* Hikes are also offered by the *Highland Outdoor Tours, Tel. 438 8069.*

Taxis have no meters, but for the most popular routes the fares are fixed. Generally, these are posted in the hotels. If not, ask the receptionist. It is nevertheless advisable to know some of the fares by heart; for less popular routes, agree on the price first. Normally, Bajan taxi drivers are quite honest and will not try to take advantage of you, but now and then (especially late at night) they will try to get a few extra dollars. The main guidelines are: every kilometre or fraction thereof costs 1.50 Bds$. The approximate fare from the international airport to St Lawrence is 20 Bds$, to Bridgetown 30 Bds$ and to Holetown and the west coast 38 Bds$. For some, it is also possible to rent a taxi for the entire day and let the driver explain the sights of the island to you. The *Tourist Authority* works together with the *Barbados Transport Co-op Society.* Day trips cost about 150 Bds$. *Durants, Christ Church, Tel. 428 65 65 and 428 09 53, Fax 428 98 11*

## TAXES

The V.A.T. tax is 15 per cent and is added to almost everything. Larger hotels are only allowed to charge a reduced rate of 7.5 per cent.

## TELEPHONE

A local call – meaning a call to all the villages on the island – costs 25 cents from a public telephone. You can also purchase telephone cards

---

### Open house programme

Barbados is proud of its beautiful, old plantation houses, but only few are open to the public as museums. During the winter months, it is nevertheless possible to visit one of these private houses on a certain day of the week and get to know the current owners. The programme varies from month to month. Please check the tourism information brochures for the exact times and days.

in the supermarkets and in the mini markets of the petrol stations.

When you hear the dial tone, start dialling
– *for Canada: 011 1*
– *for the USA: 011 1,*
– *for the U.K.: 011 44*
then dial the code of the place you wish to reach but without the zero. The area code for Barbados is *246*, the international dialling code is *001*.

## TELEVISION & RADIO

Barbados has its own, government-owned television station called *Caribbean Broadcasting Corporation* (CBC), which also sends its signals to the neighbouring islands of St Lucia, Grenada, St Vincent and the Grenadines. Four additional channels, among them CNN, can be received via satellite.

On AM and FM, a total of five radio channels broadcast their signals: the government-owned stations CBC (900 KHZ AM) and Radio Liberty (98.1 MHZ FM); additionally, the Voice of Barbados (VOB, AM), Barbados Broadcasting Service (BBS, FM) and Yess Ten Four (AM).

## TIME ZONES

The time difference between Central European Time (CET) and Barbados time is minus six hours in the summer and minus five hours in the winter.

## TIPPING

Generally, a 10 per cent service charge is added to the restaurant bill. Depending on the service you got, round off the figure upwards or downwards. Sometimes you will notice that the service charge is missing, in which case leave a tip of at least 10 per cent.

## TOURIST INFORMATION

### Barbados Tourism Authority

In Canada:
*105 Adelaide Street West, Suite 1010, Toronto, Ontario M5H 1P9, Tel. (416) 214 98 80; Fax (416) 214 98 82, www.barbados.org, e-mail btapublic@globalserve.net*

In the U.K.:
*263 Tottenham Court Road, London W1P 0LA, Tel. (0171) 636 94 48, Fax (0171) 637 14 96, www.barbados.org, e-mail barbadosuk@aol.com*

In the USA:
*800 Second Avenue, 2nd Floor, New York, NY 10017, Tel. (212) 986 65 16 or toll-free (USA only): (1800) 221 98 31, Fax (212) 573 98 50, www.barbados.org, e-mail blany @worldnet.att.net*

## VILLAS

Apart from hotels and holiday flats of all categories, it is also possible to rent whole houses and villas. The selection is a large one, ranging from modest wooden houses to elegant plantation homes. Most of the time, the price includes the services of a maid and a cook.

### Bajan Services

Only really exclusive villas on the west coast at a price of between 100 and about 500 US$ per day are offered for rent from this company. Please ask for the *Villa Guide*. *Sea-scape Cottage, Gibbs, St Peter, Tel. 422 26 18, Fax 422 53 66, www.bajanservices.com*

**Alleyne Aguilar & Altman**
*Derricks, St James, Tel. 432 08 40, Fax 432 21 47, e-mail villas@carib surf.com*

## Guide by side

This young travel agency run by Austrians has specialized in getting the right accommodations for European individual travellers. *Sandrina Prisching, 'Hy-A-Lea', Dover Gardens, Christ Church, Tel./Fax 420 21 35, e-mail sanravi@sunbeach.net*

VOLTAGE

Voltage is 110 volts; it is recommended to bring appliances that allow you to switch the voltage. You need an American-style flat plug for connecting your appliances.

# WEATHER IN BRIDGETOWN

*Seasonal averages*

**Daytime temperatures in °C/F**

| Jan | Feb | Mar | April | May | June | July | Aug | Sept | Oct | Nov | Dec |
|---|---|---|---|---|---|---|---|---|---|---|---|
| 28/82 | 28/82 | 29/84 | 30/86 | 31/88 | 31/88 | 30/86 | 31/88 | 31/88 | 30/86 | 29/84 | 28/82 |

**Night-time temperatures in °C/F**

| Jan | Feb | Mar | April | May | June | July | Aug | Sept | Oct | Nov | Dec |
|---|---|---|---|---|---|---|---|---|---|---|---|
| 21/70 | 21/70 | 21/70 | 22/72 | 23/73 | 23/73 | 23/73 | 23/73 | 23/73 | 23/73 | 23/73 | 22/72 |

**Sunshine: hours per day**

| Jan | Feb | Mar | April | May | June | July | Aug | Sept | Oct | Nov | Dec |
|---|---|---|---|---|---|---|---|---|---|---|---|
| 8 | 9 | 9 | 9 | 9 | 8 | 9 | 9 | 8 | 7 | 8 | 8 |

**Rainfall: days per month**

| Jan | Feb | Mar | April | May | June | July | Aug | Sept | Oct | Nov | Dec |
|---|---|---|---|---|---|---|---|---|---|---|---|
| 13 | 8 | 8 | 7 | 9 | 14 | 18 | 16 | 15 | 15 | 16 | 14 |

**Ocean temperatures in °C/F**

| Jan | Feb | Mar | April | May | June | July | Aug | Sept | Oct | Nov | Dec |
|---|---|---|---|---|---|---|---|---|---|---|---|
| 26/79 | 25/77 | 25/77 | 26/79 | 27/81 | 28/82 | 28/82 | 28/82 | 28/82 | 28/82 | 28/82 | 27/81 |

# Do's and don'ts

*A couple of things you should watch out for in peaceful Barbados – and your holiday will even be nicer*

## Poisonous trees

The tropical flora of the island is beautiful, but there is one lurking trap in the form of the *manchineel tree*, whose sap drips down from it after a shower. The sap is poisonous and has an abrasive effect on the skin. So keep your distance as soon as the first drops start falling. Signs warn passers-by of the danger, and in case they are overlooked, the trunk of the tree has a red band around it. Even if it doesn't rain, the leaves shouldn't be pulled off so the caustic sap can't drip out. And don't touch the small, green fruit – it is poisonous as well. The manchineels are common on beaches, especially in the north-western coast. As fantastic as it sounds, the tree is one big poison jar!

## Inappropriate clothing

To put it mildly, Bajans are not amused when tourists walk around in their beach clothes in the capital or inside a supermarket. Even worse: walk by a church wearing only a bikini or swimming trunks! So please remember to wear beach clothing only in beaches.

All of the better hotels encourage their guests to dress in *casual elegance* after 6 pm. The gentlemen who would like to go out for dinner should wear long trousers and at the very least a short sleeved T-Shirt; in the more elegant restaurants it is expected that the trousers won't be blue jeans. Shorts, including more formal Bermudas, are not evening clothes in Barbados. However, only the most exclusive restaurants and official receptions will require a jacket and tie. Even the nightclubs for young people will deny admission to men wearing tank tops. The ladies have it easier; they can go out in the evening wearing a light summer dress or dinner shorts. However, they should also take care not to show too much while strolling in the city or attending a religious service.

And sorry, ladies: we have to tell you that in pious Barbados topless bathing is not only scorned, but strictly prohibited – and that includes hotel pools. In case of violation, you will get an embarrassing warning, and if the violation is repeated you will pay a fine. Nudist camps are non-existent and you should not try to swim in the nude even if the beach looks empty. In highly populated Barbados, an empty beach remains so only for a short period.

## Going out in the wrong evening

One evening in the hotel, you listen attentively as other holiday-makers tell the others about their exciting evening at the nightclub xyz. Before the evening is over, you make up your mind to pay that 'super exciting' place with the 'first-rate music' a visit. The moment you arrive, you think at first that you have come to the wrong address; it's midnight and there's still nothing going on – according to the description, the place was teeming with people at the same time.

In Barbados, an unwritten rule decides what nightclub on what evening will be 'in'. Generally speaking, that evening will be when a live band plays there. To save time and frustration, it's best to check with the Bajans themselves. Then nothing can go wrong and you will have a great, unforgettable evening dancing into the morning hours.

## Stumble into every-day traps

Never board a bus unless you have the exact change – the drivers of the blue buses don't give out any change and in the others change will only be given for small notes or coins.

Before you board a taxi, by all means negotiate the price. It's even better to find out how much taxis charge.

If you shop in a duty-free shop, be ready to show your passport (or a copy thereof) and your plane ticket. Don't be suspicious, it's just that even when the plane departs in the middle of the night your purchases will be handed over to you at the airport.

Don't underestimate the strength of the tropical sun; in the first days, expose your skin to the sun for only a few minutes, this will allow your skin to get used to the rays. Even if the sky is over-cast, there is still the danger of a sunburn, so don't forget to rub your skin with a high sun protection factor cream! When you are in the water, especially while snorkelling, wear a T-shirt for added skin protection.

## Lack of manners

Bajans are particularly courteous. Needless to say, at the very least they expect the same politeness and friendliness from you. By no means raise your voice – even if you are in a very excited state – or you will lose face and nobody will respect you any longer, something you certainly don't want to happen.

It is considered good form to accept queues and wait for your turn – like all the others. Pushing one's way to the front is considered loutish behaviour and judged accordingly.

## Being careless

Barbados is very proud of its relatively high standard of living for Caribbean standards as well as for its low crime rate, especially with regard to tourists. Those who still dare to snatch a handbag from a tourist can expect to spend up to 10 to 15 years behind bars. In spite of these draconian measures, the local press still reports about such incidents happening now and then. Therefore, the universal rule applies: don't lead anyone into temptation.

Valuables should not be left unsupervised on the beach, and they are best left in the hotel safe. It's hardly worth mentioning that you won't consider walking around showing off your valuable jewels and fat pocketbook.

# Road Atlas of Barbados

*Please refer to back cover for an overview
of this Road Atlas*

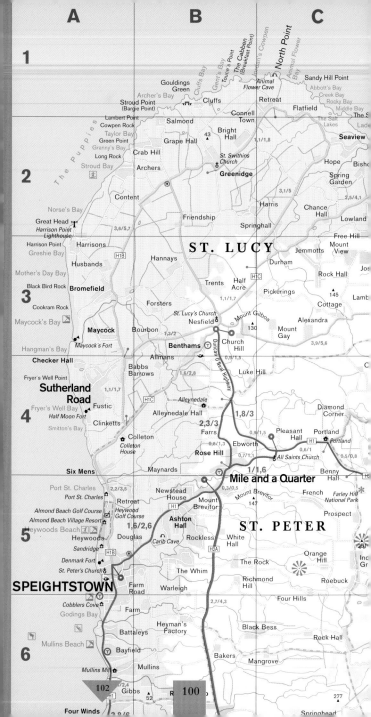

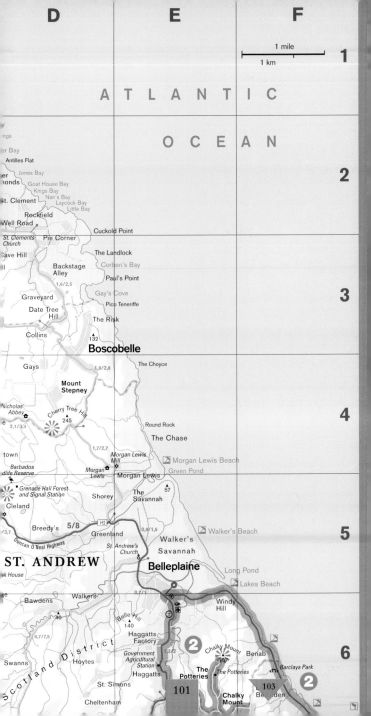

## D

ngs
or Bay
Antilles Flat
er  Jones Bay
nonds  Goat House Bay
Kings Bay
St. Clement  Nan's Bay
Laycock Bay
Little Bay
Rockfield
Well Road
St. Clements  Pie Corner
Church
Cave Hill
Backstage
Alley  1,6/2,5
Graveyard
Date Tree
Hill
Collins
Gays
▲ 132
**Boscobelle**
Mount
Stepney
1,8/2,8
Nicholas'  Cherry Tree Hill
Abbey
e  ▲ 245
2,1/3,4
town
Barbados
dlife Reserve
*Grenade Hall Forest*
*and Signal Station*
Morgan  Morgan Lewis
Cleland  Lewis
1,7/2,7
Shorey
Breedy's  5/8
Duncan O'Neal Highway  Greenland
3,7
k House
ST. ANDREW
Bawdens  Walkers
40
4,7/7,5
Swanns  Hoytes
Scotland District  St. Simons
Cheltenham

## E

Cuckold Point
The Landlock
Corben's Bay
Paul's Point
Gay's Cove
Pico Teneriffe
The Risk
The Choyce
Round Rock
The Chase
Morgan Lewis
Mill
Morgan Lewis
Green Pond
The
Savannah  ▲ 57
0,9/1,5
St. Andrew's
Church
Belle Hill
▲ 140
Haggatts
Factory
*Government*
*Agricultural*
*Station*
Haggatts
Walker's
Savannah
**Belleplaine**
Long Pond
Lakes Beach
0,7/1
Windy
Hill
1,3/2
Chalky Mount
The
Potteries  *The Potteries*
Chalky
Mount
Benab
**101**

## F

ATLANTIC

OCEAN

Morgan Lewis Beach

Walker's Beach

Barclays Park

Benab...den

**103**

1 mile
1 km

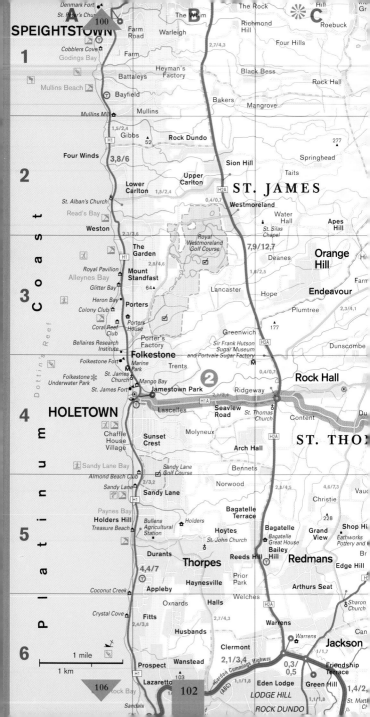

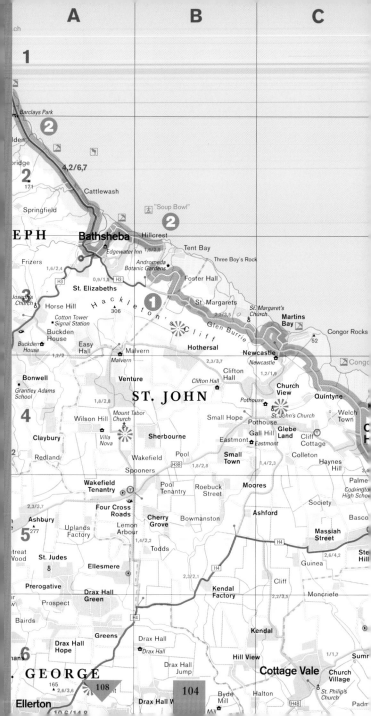

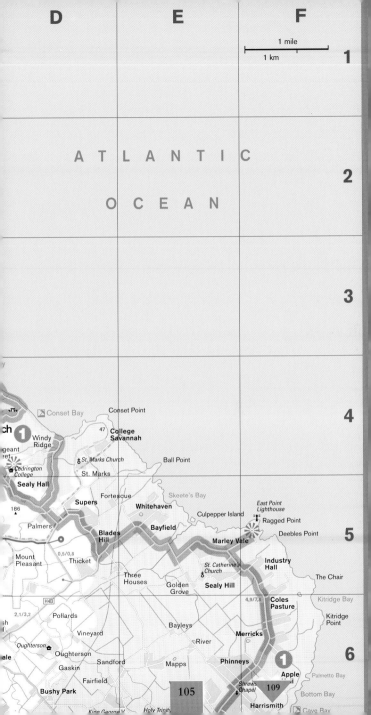

1 mile

1 km

1

A T L A N T I C

2

O C E A N

3

Conset Bay    Conset Point

4

Windy
Ridge          47   College
Savannah

geant
eet          St. Marks Church      Ball Point

Cedrington
College        St. Marks

Sealy Hall

Fortescue

186          Supers      Whitehaven          East Point
Lighthouse

Palmers                                  Culpepper Island   Ragged Point

Blades                Bayfield                        Deebles Point
Hill                              Marley Vale

5

Mount        0,5/0,8                                  Industry
Pleasant     Thicket                                 Hall          The Chair

Three        St. Catherine's
Houses       Church

Golden    Sealy Hill
Grove

H4B                                        4,9/7,8   Coles          Kitridge Bay
Pasture
2,1/3,2      Pollards                                              Kitridge
Point

Vineyard              Bayleys          Merricks

Oughterson                              River                      6
ale          Oughterson                                Phinneys

Gaskin      Sandford    Mapps                          Apple    Palmetto Bay

Fairfield                          Shrews          109   Bottom Bay
Bushy Park                         Chapel
King George V   Holy Trinity              Harrismith   Cave Bay

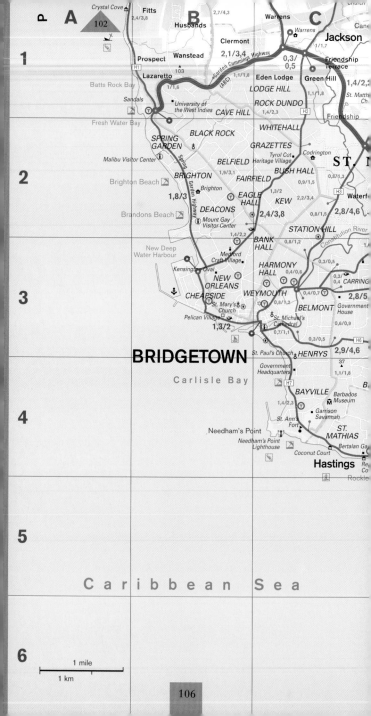

Crystal Cove

**102**

Fitts

Husbands

Warrens

Warrens

Jackson

Cane

Church

1/1,7

Clermont

**2,1/3,4**

Prospect

Wanstead

Garden Cummings Highway (ABC)

0,3/0,5

Friendship Terrace

Green Hill

Lazaretto

1/1,6

103

1,1/1,8

Eden Lodge

**1,4/2,**

LODGE HILL

1,1/1,8

St. Matthe
Ch

Batts Rock Bay

Sandals

University of
the West Indies

ROCK DUNDO

CAVE HILL

1,4/2,3

Friendship

Fresh Water Bay

WHITEHALL

SPRING
GARDEN

BLACK ROCK

GRAZETTES

ST. M

Malibu Visitor Center

BELFIELD

Tyrol Cot
Heritage Village

Codrington

Brighton Beach

BRIGHTON

1,9/3,1

FAIRFIELD

BUSH HALL

0,9/1,5

0,8/1,3

**1,8/3**

Brighton

EAGLE
HALL

1,3/2

KEW

2,2/3,4

H3

Waterf

Brandons Beach

DEACONS

Mount Gay
Visitor Center

**2,4/3,8**

0,8/1,5

**2,8/4,6**

New Deep
Water Harbour

Kensington Oval

1,4/2,2

BANK
HALL

0,8/1,2

STATION
HILL

Constitution River

1,

Medford
Craft Village

NEW
ORLEANS

HARMONY
HALL

0,4/0,6

0,3/0,5

CHEAPSIDE

WEYMOUTH

0,8/1,2

0,3/
0,4

CARRING

St. Mary's
Church

Pelican Village

BELMONT

0,4/0,7

**2,8/5**

**1,3/2**

St. Michael's
Cathedral

Government
House

0,6/0,9

0,7/1,1

0,3/0,5

H6

**BRIDGETOWN**

St. Paul's Church

HENRYS

**2,9/4,6**

Carlisle Bay

Government
Headquarters

37

1,1/1,8

H7

BAYVILLE

Barbados
Museum

B

1,4/2,3

St. Ann's
Fort

Garrison
Savannah

Needham's Point

ST.
MATHIAS

Needham's Point
Lighthouse

Bertalan Ga

Coconut Court

**Hastings**

Re
Co

Rockle

**5**

C a r i b b e a n    S e a

**6**

1 mile

1 km

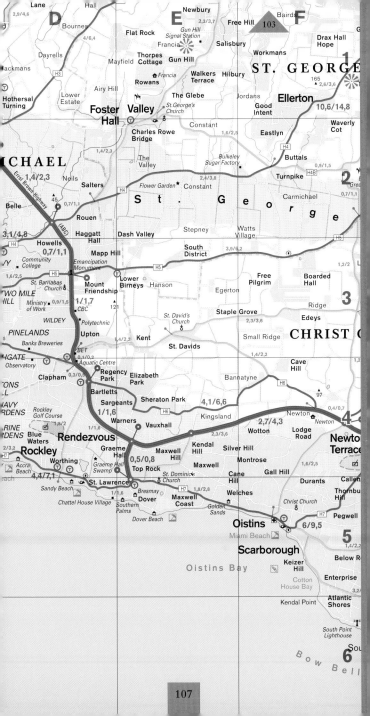

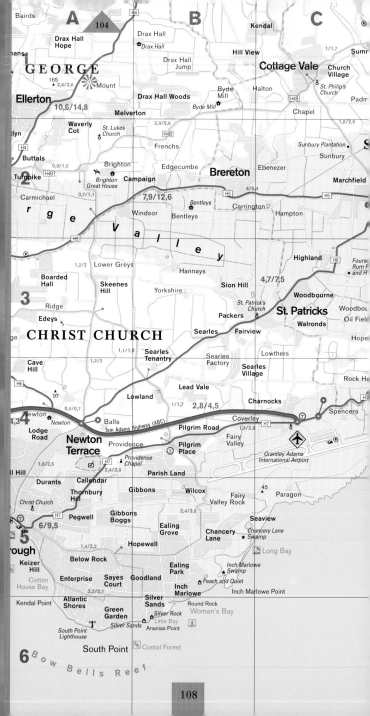

# ROAD ATLAS LEGEND

| | |
|---|---|
| Dual carriage-way with motorway characteristics<br>Autobahnähnliche Schnellstraße<br>Double chaussée de type autoroutier<br>Doppia carreggiata di tipo autostradale<br>Autovía | Church • Chapel<br>Kirche • Kapelle<br>Église • Chapelle<br>Chiesa • Cappella<br>Iglesia • Capilla |
| Highway<br>Fernverkehrsstraße<br>Grande route de transit<br>Strada di transito<br>Autovía | Castle • Ruin<br>Burg • Ruine<br>Château • Ruines<br>Castello • Rovine<br>Castillo • Ruina |
| Important main road<br>Wichtige Hauptstraße<br>Route de comm. importante<br>Strada di interesse regionale<br>Carretera general importante | Point of interest • Nature sight<br>Sehenswürdigkeit • Naturattraktion<br>Curiosité • Curiosité naturelle<br>Curiosità • Curiosità natural<br>Curiosidad • Curiosidad natural |
| Main road<br>Hauptstraße<br>Route principale<br>Strada principale<br>Carretera principal | Windmill • Cave<br>Windmühle • Höhle<br>Moulin à vent • Grotte<br>Mulino a vento • Grotta<br>Molino de viento • Cueva |
| Secondary road<br>Nebenstraße<br>Route secondaire<br>Strada secondaria<br>Carretera secundaria | Hotel • Plantation house<br>Hotel • Plantagenhaus<br>Hôtel • Maison de plantation<br>Albergo • Casa di piantagione<br>Hotel • Casa de plantación |
| Carriage way • Path<br>Fahrweg • Pfad<br>Chemin carrossable • Sentier<br>Strada carrozzabile • Sentiero<br>Camino vecinal • Sendero | Wildlife reserve • Riding<br>Wildgehege • Reiten<br>Parc à gibier • Centre équestre<br>Bandita di caccia • Equitazione<br>Reserve de caza • Paseos a caballo |
| 1,4/2,3 Distance in miles/km<br>Entfernung in miles/km<br>Distance en miles/km<br>Distanze in miles/km<br>Distancia en miles/km | Lighthouse • Radio Tower<br>Leuchtturm • Funkturm<br>Phare • Pylône de radio<br>Faro • Torre della radio<br>Faro • Repetidor |
| Parish boundary<br>Kirchengemeindegrenzen<br>Frontière de paroisse<br>Confine di parrocchia<br>Frontera de parroquia | Picnic area • Shipwreck<br>Picknick • Schiffswrack<br>Pique-nique • Épave de bateau<br>Picnic • Relitto di nave<br>Picknick • Barco naufragado |
| Int. Airport • Harbour<br>Int. Flughafen • Hafen<br>Aéroport int. • Port<br>Aeroporto int. • Porto<br>Aeropuerto int. • Puerto | Beach • Yachting<br>Strand • Segelsport<br>Plage • Centre de voile<br>Spiaggia • Sport velico<br>Playa • Deporte de vela |
| Museum • Monument<br>Museum • Denkmal<br>Musée • Monument<br>Museo • Monumento<br>Museo • Monumento | Deap sea fishing • Scuba diving<br>Hochseefischen • Sporttauchen<br>Pêche de haute mer • Sous-marine plongée<br>Pesca d'alto mare • Sport subacqueo<br>Pesca de altura • Submarinisimo |
| Synagogue • Market<br>Synagoge • Markt<br>Synagogue • Marché<br>Sinagoga • Mercato<br>Sinagoga • Mercado | Parasailing • Windsurfing<br>Paragleiten • Windsurfen<br>Parasailing • Planche à voile<br>Parasailing • Surfing<br>Parapente • Windsurf |
| Information • Police<br>Information • Polizei<br>Informations • Police<br>Informazione • Polizia<br>Información • Policía | Golf • National park<br>Golf • Nationalpark<br>Golf • Parc national<br>Golf • Parco nazionale<br>Golf • Parque nacional |
| Post office • Hospital<br>Postamt • Krankenhaus<br>Poste • Hôpital<br>Posta • Ospedale<br>Oficina de correos • Hospital | Petrol station<br>Tankstelle<br>Station essence<br>Stazione di rifornimento<br>Estación de servicio |

1 mile

1 km

# INDEX

*The index lists all the places and main sights mentioned in this guide. Bold page numbers indicate the main entry, italics indicate photos.*

## Hotels

# What do you get for your money?

The Barbadian dollar is firmly linked to the US dollar. In hotels, for one American dollar you get between 1.95 to 1.98 Bds$.

For the visitor it is important to know what to expect to pay for eating and drinking, souvenirs and car rental. The following average prices should give you a rough idea of what your money is worth:

For a dinner, expect to pay from 12 to 65 Bds$. The average price for a glass of rum punch is 4.50 to 5 Bds$. A local beer costs between 3 and 5 Bds$, a glass of wine 7 to 9 Bds$. If you intend to buy souvenirs: the one-litre bottle of Mount Gay Eclipse rum costs about 12.60 Bds$, the older Cockspur V. S. O. R. Fine Rum in the 750-ml-bottle can be had for 18 Bds$.

Generally, high-quality cosmetics are reasonably priced. A bottle of pure aloe vera (to protect you against sunburn) costs about 12.80 Bds$ in the supermarket, a tube of toothpaste starts at 1.80 Bds$. A packet of cigarettes from the vending machine sets you back 6 to 9 Bds$. A hired car with fully comprehensive insurance can be had for approx. 110 Bds$ per day, a week costs about 460 Bds$. You shoould expect to pay approximately 100 Bds$ per person for a day trip.

| Bds$ | £ | US$ | Can$ |
|---|---|---|---|
| 1 | 0.31 | 0.51 | 0.75 |
| 2 | 0.62 | 1.02 | 1.50 |
| 3 | 0.93 | 1.53 | 2.25 |
| 4 | 1.24 | 2.55 | 3.00 |
| 5 | 1.55 | 2.55 | 3.75 |
| 6 | 1.86 | 3.06 | 4.50 |
| 7 | 2.17 | 3.57 | 5.25 |
| 8 | 2.48 | 4.08 | 6.00 |
| 9 | 2.79 | 4.59 | 6.75 |
| 10 | 3.10 | 5.10 | 7.50 |
| 15 | 4.65 | 7.65 | 11.25 |
| 20 | 6.20 | 10.20 | 15.00 |
| 25 | 7.75 | 12.75 | 18.75 |
| 30 | 9.30 | 15.30 | 22.50 |
| 40 | 12.40 | 20.40 | 30.00 |
| 50 | 15.50 | 25.50 | 37.50 |
| 75 | 23.25 | 38.25 | 56.25 |
| 100 | 31.00 | 51.00 | 75.00 |
| 250 | 77.50 | 127.50 | 187.50 |
| 500 | 155.00 | 255.00 | 375.00 |
| 1,000 | 310.00 | 510.00 | 750.00 |